Handbook on Teacher Portfolios for Evaluation and Professional Development

Pamela D. Tucker

James H. Stronge

Christopher R. Gareis

EYE ON EDUCATION
6 DEPOT WAY WEST, SUITE 106
LARCHMONT, NY 10538
(914) 833–0551
(914) 833–0761 fax
www.eyeoneducation.com

Library of Congress Cataloging-in-Publication Data

Tucker, Pamela D.
Handbook on teacher portfolios for evaluation & professional development / by Pamela D. Tucker, James H. Stronge, Christopher R. Gareis.
p.cm.
Includes bibliographical references and index.
ISBN 1-930556-32-2
1. Portfolios in education—United States—Handbooks, manuals, etc. 2. Teachers—Rating of—United States—Handbooks, manuals, etc. 3. Teachers—In-service training—United States—Handbooks, manuals, etc. I. Stronge, James H. II. Gareis, Christopher R. III. Title.

LB1728.T83 2002
371.14′4—dc21   2001058509

10 9 8 7 6 5 4 3 2 1

Dedication

To Larry, Mike, Jeff, and Alissa
To Terri, Tim, and Beth
To Molly, Hance, and Isabelle
For your continuing inspiration and support

Editorial and production services provided by
Richard H. Adin Freelance Editorial Services
52 Oakwood Blvd., Poughkeepsie, NY 12603-4112
(845-471-3566)

ABOUT THE COMPANION COMPACT DISK

Our purpose in writing this book was to provide structure and guidance to educators as they design, develop, and use teacher portfolios. Many of the materials we have developed in our work with various school systems are included as hard copy in the appendices and as easy-to-modify documents on a companion compact disk. For your convenience in organizing portfolios as suggested in this book, you are encouraged to copy and adapt the templates on the CD in *Microsoft Word*. Also available on the CD are figures and tables from the book which can be viewed with *Adobe Acrobat Reader*. The contents of the CD are listed below.

Instructions

- Copy the entire contents of the CD-ROM to a new folder on your hard drive called "Teacher Portfolio Eye On Ed."

- The CD-ROM features both templates and figures. The templates can be modified and customized to fit the needs of your school or district in *Microsoft Word*.

- To view the figures, you need *Adobe Acrobat Reader*, a program that can be downloaded from the Internet at no charge from www.adobe.com/products/acrobat/readstep2.html

- *Please note:* The contents of the CD-ROM may not be accessible by older versions of Macintosh software.

- If you need assistance, please contact your school's Technology Coordinator.

Figures on the CD

♦ Teacher portfolio uses (Figure 1.2)

This *Adobe Acrobat* file lists the possible low-stakes and high-stakes uses of portfolios.

♦ Four essential physical features of teacher portfolios (Figure 2.5)

This *Adobe Acrobat* file provides an easy reference guide on the key features of a teacher portfolio with a rationale for each.

♦ Types of artifacts grouped by category (Figure 2.8)

This *Adobe Acrobat* file provides a list of portfolio artifacts grouped by who produced them and for what purpose.

♦ General model for the portfolio process (Figure 3.1)

This *Adobe Acrobat* file depicts the steps in developing and using a portfolio.

♦ Teacher evaluation data sources matrix (Figure 4.3)

This *Adobe Acrobat* file lists possible data sources for teacher evaluation based on the major performance domains.

♦ Prospective contributors to a teaching portfolio (Figure 5.2)

This *Adobe Acrobat* file describes the role various people can play in making contributions to a teacher's portfolio development and use.

♦ Sources and examples of reflective prompts (Figure 5.5)

This *Adobe Acrobat* file offers a sampling of questions to help the teacher in selecting, organizing, and explaining the artifacts to be used in a portfolio.

♦ Benefits in using teacher portfolios (Figure 6.1)

This *Adobe Acrobat* file lists the primary benefits of teacher portfolios in their use for evaluation and professional development.

♦ Possible liabilities in using teacher portfolios (Figure 6.2)

This *Adobe Acrobat* file lists possible drawbacks to the use of teacher portfolios in their use for evaluation and professional development.

♦ Guiding questions for the use of portfolios (Figure 6.3)

This *Adobe Acrobat* file provides a list of key considerations in the development of a system using teacher portfolios.

Templates on the CD

♦ Performance standards (Appendix A)

This *Microsoft Word* file describes a three-tiered framework of performance standards for teachers and provides a sample set of performance domains, standards, and indicators.

♦ Performance assessment rubrics (Appendix B)

This *Microsoft Word* file describes the purpose of a performance assessment rubric and provides a sample rubric that is linked to the performance standards given in the "perfstand.doc" document.

♦ General guidelines for organizing a teacher portfolio (Appendix C)

This *Microsoft Word* file provides general guidelines on the development of a portfolio and a listing of sample activities for documenting standards in each of the major performance domains. A sample caption form is also included in these materials for describing and commenting upon selected artifacts.

♦ Performance standards cross-referenced with sample artifacts (Appendix D)

This *Microsoft Word* file provides a listing of 57 sample artifacts for documenting the cross-referenced performance standards.

♦ Sample artifacts cross-referenced with performance standards (Appendix E)

This *Microsoft Word* file provides a listing of sample artifacts to document performance standards organized by the four major performance domains.

♦ Portfolio feedback form (Appendix F)

This *Microsoft Word* file provides a feedback form that could be used with teachers to note the presence of evidence for each of the performance standards along with comments.

♦ Client surveys (Appendix G)

This *Microsoft Word* file provides a description of student surveys, sample forms for three different grade ranges, and guiding questions to summarize survey data.

♦ Public dissemination plan (Appendix H)

This *Microsoft Word* file provides a sample work plan for disseminating information about a new approach to teacher evaluation.

- Sample newsletters introducing the concept of portfolios (Appendix I)

  This *Microsoft Word* file provides a sequence of three sample newsletters that might be used to share information with the school community about changes in the evaluation system.

- Materials for evaluating the use of teacher portfolios (Appendix J)

  This *Microsoft Word* file provides sample instruments for evaluating the effectiveness of portfolios and other changes in an evaluation system.

License and Warranty

EYE ON EDUCATION grants a nonexclusive license to use the software solely for your own personal or business purposes. EYE ON EDUCATION reserves all rights not expressly granted herein. EYE ON EDUCATION is the owner of all rights, title, and interests, including copyright, in and to the compilation of the Software. Copyright to the individual programs recorded on the Software Media is owned by the author or other authorized copyright owner of each program. Ownership of the Software and all proprietary rights relating thereto remain with EYE ON EDUCATION and its licensers.

EYE ON EDUCATION warrants that the Software and Software Media are free from defects in materials and workmanship under normal use for a period of thirty (30) days from the date of purchase of this Book. If EYE ON EDUCATION receives notification within the warranty period of defects in materials or workmanship, EYE ON EDUCATION will replace the defective Software Media. EYE ON EDUCATION and the authors of this book disclaim other warranties, expressed or implied, including without limitation implied warranties of merchantability and fitness for a particular purpose with respect to the software and files, and/or the techniques described in this book. EYE ON EDUCATION does not warrant that the functions contained in the software will meet your requirements or that the operation of the software will be error free.

Also Available from EYE ON EDUCATION

Teacher Retention:
What is Your Weakest Link?
India Podsen

Coaching and Mentoring
First-Year and Student Teachers
India Podsen and Vicki Denmark

Staff Development: Practices That Promote
Leadership in Learning Communities
Sally Zepeda

Human Resources Administration:
A School-based Perspective 2/e
Richard E. Smith

Motivating and Inspiring Teachers:
The Educator's Guide for Building Staff Morale
Todd Whitaker, Beth Whitaker, and Dale Lumpa

Dealing with Difficult Teachers
Todd Whitaker

The Emerging Principalship
Linda Skrla, David Erlandson, etc.

Money and Schools, 2/e
David C. Thompson and R. Craig Wood

Introduction to Educational
Leadership and Organizational Behavior
Patti L. Chance and Edward W. Chance

Thinking Through the Principalship
Dianne E. Ashby and Samuel E. Krug

Dealing with Difficult Parents
Todd Whitaker and Douglas J. Fiore

Creating Connections for Better Schools:
How Leaders Enhance School Culture
Douglas J. Fiore

ACKNOWLEDGMENTS

Our research regarding teacher portfolios has its genesis in discussions with teachers and administrators about advancing the teaching profession and in our work with a number of school districts that have sought to employ portfolios to improve teacher practice. In particular, we are finding that increasing numbers of school districts desire to simultaneously elevate teacher accountability and teacher professional growth. One vehicle for tackling these dual purposes is the use of teacher portfolios as a key component in a more comprehensive teacher evaluation and professional development system. Through collaboration with teachers and administrators, we have attempted to bridge the conceptual aspects of teacher portfolios with what is feasible and useful for educators who want to improve existing practices for both professional growth and performance evaluation.

We would like to extend our sincere appreciation to all of the individuals and organizations that supported and assisted us in this effort. In particular, we wish to acknowledge the following school districts in our home state of Virginia for their efforts to improve teacher practice through performance evaluation and professional growth systems that incorporate many of the components we recommend in this book: Alexandria City Schools, Dinwiddie County Schools, Hampton City Schools, Roanoke City Schools, and Williamsburg-James City County Schools. We drew from their practice to highlight selected concepts and, in some instances, to offer illustrations and materials included in appendices. We are grateful to these and the many school systems from across the country that shared their evaluation procedures and instruments with us.

Just as the content of this handbook reflects the efforts of many people, so does its organization, research, and editing. We wish to thank Bud Livers for his work on the various appendices included in the book, Daphne Keiser for her collection of relevant quotations and organization of references, and Whitney Sherman for her assistance with the literature search. We appreciate the considerable time and effort they all invested in the project.

Pamela D. Tucker
James H. Stronge
Christopher R. Gareis

TABLE OF CONTENTS

ABOUT THE AUTHORS

Pamela D. Tucker is an assistant professor of education in the Curry School of Education at the University of Virginia and serves as the director of the Principal Internship Program. She has worked with numerous school systems in the development of new evaluation systems and recently served as one of the facilitators for the development of Virginia's *Guidelines for Uniform Performance Standards and Evaluation Criteria for Teachers, Administrators, and Superintendents*. Her research focuses on various aspects of personnel evaluation and the nature of the school principalship. Books coauthored with others include, *Evaluation Handbook for Professional Support Personnel* (Center for Research on Educational Accountability and Teacher Evaluation), and *Teacher Evaluation and Student Achievement* (National Education Association). Articles address topics such as the "Legal Context for Teacher Evaluation," "Helping Struggling Teachers," and "Guidelines for Linking Student Achievement to Teacher Evaluation." As a special education teacher and former administrator in a school for learning disabled students, she has worked with a variety of student populations and has a particular concern for students who are most at-risk for school failure. She earned her EdD in Educational Administration from the College of William and Mary.

James H. Stronge is Heritage Professor in the Educational Policy, Planning, and Leadership Area at the College of William and Mary, Williamsburg, Virginia. One of his primary research interests is in educational personnel evaluation. He has worked with numerous school districts and other educational organizations to design and develop evaluation systems for teachers, administrators, and support personnel. He is the author or coauthor of numerous articles, books, and technical reports on teacher, administrator, and support personnel evaluation. Selected authored or edited publications include the books, *Evaluating Professional Support Personnel in Education* (Sage Publications), *Evaluation Handbook for Professional Support Personnel* (Center for Research on Educational Accountability and Teacher Evaluation), *Evaluating Teaching: A Guide to Current Thinking and Best Practice* (Corwin Press), and *Teacher Evaluation and Student Achievement* (National Education Association). Most recently, he developed the *Handbook on Teacher Effectiveness* for the Association for Supervision and Curriculum Development. Dr. Stronge also served as director of the Evaluating Professional Support Personnel project conducted by the Center for Research on Educational Accountability and Teacher Evaluation (CREATE). Currently, he is

Associate Editor of the *Journal of Personnel Evaluation in Education*. His doctorate in the area of educational administration and planning was received from the University of Alabama. He has been a teacher, counselor, and district-level administrator.

Christopher R. Gareis is Associate Dean for Professional Services in the School of Education at the College of William and Mary. He has worked with school divisions and education leaders in the area of personnel evaluation, with particular interest in the role of portfolios. In addition to this area, Dr. Gareis' research interests include educational planning, program evaluation, and the principalship. As a former schoolteacher and principal, he has worked with a broad spectrum of student populations, faculties, and communities. These experiences lend special weight to Dr. Gareis' role in teacher and principal preparation and in creating partnerships to address the challenges of teacher training and professional development. He earned a doctorate in educational administration from the College of William and Mary.

PREFACE

What does it mean to be a teacher? How do we nourish and develop the level of teacher quality and professionalism that our schools so desperately need? How do we provide the support and guidance that teachers need so that they, in turn, can help students? The challenges for educators have never been greater as they take responsibility for helping *all* students reach high academic goals. Ensuring teacher quality involves a range of strategies from the quality of training for pre-service teachers to quality of life issues for practicing teachers. Teachers' efforts must be recognized and sustained in the challenging task of meeting the educational needs of a diverse student population.

We believe that portfolios have the potential to provide a more personal and meaningful approach to the ongoing analysis of daily practice, and we advocate the use of portfolios as a tool for teachers and administrators to:

- encourage a reflective approach to teaching
- facilitate instructionally focused dialogue with colleagues and supervisors
- examine and define their own professional development
- document their professional duties as a teacher.

We believe portfolios can help teachers consider what works and doesn't work, how to improve practice, and how to capture the impact of teaching on students.

Although portfolios can be used for a wide variety of purposes and for teachers at any developmental stage (e.g., pre-service, novice, master, and nationally-recognized), in the *Handbook on Teacher Portfolios for Evaluation and Professional Development*, we focus on their use by practicing teachers for the primary purposes of evaluation and professional development. In Chapter 1, "Handbook on Teacher Portfolios: An Introduction," we define what we mean by a portfolio, what it has to offer the professional educator, and how it can be used for evaluation and professional development. Three case studies of how portfolios can be used at the national and local level are highlighted at the end of this chapter. In Chapter 2, "Developing a Teacher Portfolio," we offer very specific guidance to the individual teacher on how to structure and develop an effective portfolio. Chapter 3, "Putting Portfolios into Action," provides a broader perspective on what to consider in the implementation of portfolios as a school or school system.

In Chapter 4, "Teacher Portfolios and Teacher Evaluation," and Chapter 5, "Teacher Portfolios and Professional Development," we explore the use of portfolios for the two different, but interrelated, purposes of evaluation and professional development. From our perspective, evaluation without professional development or growth serves no purpose, just as professional development without any assessment of its impact has no meaning. We believe that in a supportive, trusting supervisory climate, the two purposes can go hand in hand.

In the final chapter, Chapter 6, "The Role of Portfolios for the Teaching Profession," we summarize what the educational community has learned about portfolios and what are future directions for portfolios. In the appendices, an introduction suggests how to use the various resources in the handbook for your specific needs. Included in the appendices are tools to help you structure the portfolio, decide what to include, organize the contents, include student feedback, and implement at the district level. Feel free to copy and adapt the materials found in the appendices. An electronic version of them can be found on the companion CD to assist you in getting started with a portfolio.

As a final note, we'd like to acknowledge the truly revolutionary nature of portfolios. For the past century, the work of teachers has been inspected and monitored like that of blue-collar workers. In the last few years, portfolios have given teachers a voice in selecting, presenting, and interpreting the work that they do as professionals. Portfolios have changed the paradigm, taking teachers from a passive role in evaluation and professional development to an active one—a professional one. This shift is long overdue.

1

HANDBOOK ON TEACHER PORTFOLIOS: AN INTRODUCTION

There are two ways of spreading light:
to be the candle or the mirror that reflects it.
Edith Wharton

Portfolios, when used in the ways described in this *Handbook on Teacher Portfolios*, can help teachers monitor and improve their own performance, can assist administrators or peer evaluators in acquiring a fuller and more accurate portrait of teacher performance, and, ultimately, can benefit students in improved instructional delivery and learning opportunities. Portfolios have been used extensively with students for the same reasons that they appeal to adults. They offer a more personal, constructivist approach to documenting, reviewing, and guiding one's own learning. They are a means of linking and critically examining both the processes of your teaching and the student products that result from your efforts. They offer a means of making clear the instructional relationships among lesson plans, assessments, and student work.

In this introductory chapter, we offer an explanation of how powerful teacher portfolios can be as a tool for professionals. Specifically, we will address:

- ◆ Why teacher portfolios?
- ◆ What is a teacher portfolio?
- ◆ What is the portfolio's value for teacher evaluation?
- ◆ What is the portfolio's value for professional development?

We begin by offering a brief glimpse at why there is a growing demand for teacher portfolios.

Why Teacher Portfolios?

In the past several years, portfolios have gained increasing support for their use with students, teachers, and school administrators. Portfolios, as collections of work, have been used for centuries in the fields of art and architecture. Using a loose definition of portfolios, teachers have used them to document student learning, at least throughout this century. If we consider portfolios as the *purposeful collection of work for analysis and reflection*, however, portfolios are a relatively recent development. They were discussed in the educational literature beginning in the early 1970s as an authentic means to document student writing.[1] Within a few short years, portfolios were being considered for use with teachers.

At present, portfolios are used in a variety of settings for a variety of purposes. Teacher and administrator preparation programs are using portfolios to document the achievement of core competencies for licensure. In turn, these graduates are using portfolios to capture their formal training and their accomplishments as beginning professionals for job interviews. In Connecticut, portfolios are part of the assessment process involved in moving from an initial license to the next level of credential, a provisional license. Other states, such as Kentucky, Arizona, Indiana, and North Carolina, are also in the process of developing new assessment systems that include portfolios. Individual school systems across the country are using portfolios as a required or optional component of their evaluation processes, and individual teachers are developing portfolios for their own professional development or as a stepping-stone for National Board certification. In a similar endorsement of the concept, the Chief State School Officers have embraced the use of a "School Leaders Portfolio" as a means to evaluate the skills and knowledge of principals. Illustrative examples of how portfolios are being used successfully at the national, state, and local level are presented as case studies at the end of this chapter.

Teacher portfolios are appealing for many reasons, including their authentic nature, recognition of the complex nature or teaching, encouragement of self-reflection, and facilitation of collaborative interaction with colleagues and supervisors. In addition, the inherent flexibility and adaptability of portfolios make them an attractive vehicle for a range of purposes, particularly professional growth and evaluation. As advocates for the use of portfolios, we value the support portfolios offer teachers in examining and defining their own professional development and the central role that portfolios give teachers in the evaluation process. Portfolios embody professionalism because they encourage the reflection and self-monitoring that are hallmarks of the true professional.

What is a Teacher Portfolio?

"In its most basic form, a teaching portfolio is a collection of information about a teacher's practice."[2] Others view the teaching portfolio as a means to "demonstrate the teacher's talents," "their teaching performance," and "teaching and learning over time." These various definitions, presented in Figure 1.1, reflect differences in opinion on both the purposes of portfolios and teaching. Throughout this book, we will advocate the use of portfolios to capture the reciprocal processes of teaching and learning. The ultimate goal is to clarify, analyze, and improve the relationship between the teacher's instructional efforts and the students' learning. A teacher portfolio, therefore, is a structured collection of selected artifacts that demonstrate a teacher's competence and growth.

Figure 1.1. Teaching Portfolio Description

Authors	*Key Descriptors*
Doolittle[3]	"Just as an artist uses a portfolio of collected works to illustrate his or her talents, a teacher portfolio is designed to demonstrate the teacher's talents."
Oakley[4]	"Teachers demonstrate their teaching performance through a portfolio with multiple strands of evidence that collectively depict the teacher's approach and effectiveness at increasing student learning."
Shulman[5]	Portfolios have the "potential for documenting the unfolding of both teaching and learning over time and combining that documentation with opportunities for teachers to engage in the analysis of what they and their students have done."

What a Portfolio Is Not

Although teacher portfolios should reflect a "teacher's talents" as noted above, too heavy an emphasis on this purpose can mean the development of steamer trunks or "...scrapbooks filled with photographs of classroom life, along with affectionate notes from students and parents."[6] This approach tends not to be productive either for evaluation or professional development. We believe that an indiscriminate collection of artifacts does not encourage reflection on your practice, and provides no reasonable basis for improvement or evaluation.

Key Components of a Portfolio

For a teaching portfolio to be truly useful, it needs to be tied to clear performance expectations. We believe that if we start with *what* teachers should know and be expected to do, then we have a solid basis for documenting performance in a portfolio. By grounding the portfolio in the teacher's job responsibilities, there is a basis for comparing *actual* with *ideal* performance. In Chapter 2, we discuss the types of artifacts you might include in the portfolio and how they may be organized depending on your purpose. Typically, materials are selected that reflect instruction, student assessment, learning environment, and professionalism. One example of teacher job expectations is provided in Chapter 2, and a more detailed version, entitled "Performance Standards," appears in the appendices.

Purposes for a Teacher Portfolio

Teacher portfolios can be used for a variety of purposes, ranging from a self-analysis for the eyes of the teacher only, to a high-profile, formalized portfolio process tied to evaluation. Generally, these varied uses can be characterized as:

- ♦ low-stakes—wherein portfolios may be informal, less structured, and focused primarily on improvement; and

- ♦ high-stakes—wherein portfolios are likely to be more formal, structured, and focused on accountability.

Figure 1.2 summarizes these uses.

In the chapters that follow, we focus on the use of teaching portfolios for the two key purposes of professional development and teacher evaluation, uses that are in the realms of both low and high stakes.

Figure 1.2. Teacher Portfolio Uses

Primary Uses	*Examples*
Low-Stakes Uses	◆ Self-assessment and self-reflection
	◆ Professional development
	◆ Teacher training
	◆ Highlighting exemplary practices
	◆ Formative evaluation
High-Stakes Uses	◆ Initial hiring decisions
	◆ Teacher certification or licensure
	◆ Tenure or other personnel decisions
	◆ Documentation for remediation
	◆ Promotion and awards
	◆ Summative evaluation
	◆ Pay-for-performance plans
	◆ Advanced certification

What is the Portfolio's Value for Teacher Evaluation?[7]

We contend that portfolios do, indeed, add value to both the teacher evaluation process and the results of the evaluation. Before turning our attention to benefits from portfolio use in teacher evaluation, however, let us review problems with traditional teacher evaluation.

What's Wrong with Traditional Teacher Evaluation

Personnel evaluation in education historically has relied heavily, and often solely, on direct observation. For decades, the evaluation of teachers has consisted of a supervisor (e.g., a principal or department head), sometimes lacking specific content expertise, visiting a teacher's class once or twice a year and writing a narrative about the teacher's enthusiasm or organization. The written "evaluation" was then filed and probably never read or used again unless there were performance problems leading to termination activity.

Since the 1970s, a clinical supervision model has dominated teacher evaluation procedures. In clinical supervision, the supervisor usually met with the teacher in a pre-observation conference, observed the teacher later in the class-room, and then followed the observation with a post-observation conference in which the supervisor highlighted strengths and weaknesses of the teacher. Yet, the sole basis for performance evaluation was still the supervisor's observation. In fact, under a clinical supervision evaluation system, being observed was syn-onymous with being evaluated.

More recently, evaluation shifted its focus towards specific, research-based teaching behaviors. But how were these behaviors documented? Direct obser-vation of the teacher, and, perhaps, looking at the teacher's lesson plans, were utilized to document behaviors. Even where progressive schools experimented with peer coaching or peer evaluation, direct observation of teaching remained the central, if not the only, means of assessing a teacher's level of performance.

Whether evaluation is based on clinical supervision or "research-based" teaching behaviors, an observation-only approach to teacher evaluation results in an inspection model, leading to a deprofessionalizing of teachers. If direct ob-servation isn't a viable sole source or stand-alone method for documenting teacher performance, then what means are available to document the perfor-mance of teachers? We suggest that the use of multiple data sources, including teaching portfolios, can greatly enhance the fairness, accuracy, and comprehen-siveness of teacher performance evaluations.

What's Right with Portfolios in Teacher Evaluation

Multiple benefits accrue from the use of portfolios and other multiple data sources for evaluation. Among the numerous benefits are:

- *Expanded performance portrait*: Teacher evaluations based on portfo-lios and other data sources improve upon traditional observation-only evaluations in that the performance of the job is much more fully assessed, including both in-class and out-of-class responsibili-ties.

- *Enhanced validity*: The information used in making decisions about teachers should be a valid measure of *actual* job performance and, thus, should include information on all major dimensions of the job. By collecting information with portfolios and other forms of data, in conjunction with classroom observations, we can greatly enhance the accuracy and thoroughness of teacher evaluation.

- *Increased reliability*: Reliability (i.e., consistency or dependability) is greatly improved with a better sample of performance, and this is precisely what portfolios can provide. As compared with single-shot observations, portfolios offer a window into the classroom that can dramatically increase the reliability of the evaluation because of the larger sampling of performance from multiple perspectives.

♦ *Improved goal attainment*: If the goal of teacher evaluation is improved teacher performance and, if the goal of improved teacher performance is increased student learning, then portfolios offer a valuable aid. Portfolios offer one tool to connect

- knowledge of subject matter and curriculum to instructional planning,
- instructional planning to instructional delivery,
- instructional delivery to student assessment, and
- student assessment to actual student learning.

The goal of improved teacher-learner connections can be well documented with thoughtful, reflective portfolios.

Based on the above-noted benefits, along with others that are explored in more depth in Chapter 4, we are convinced that portfolios truly provide a value-added component to teacher evaluation.

What is the Portfolio's Value for Professional Development?

Many teachers have embraced teaching portfolios as a personal choice for their own professional development. Portfolios can capture the essence of your teaching through quiet reflection after a hectic day of nonstop action. They also provide tangible work samples that can be discussed and shared in collaborative exchanges with colleagues.

Portfolios and Teacher Self-Reflection

A teaching portfolio can be an excellent tool for learning about teaching. Whether you are a novice in the classroom or an accomplished veteran, the portfolio can serve as a constant catalyst for improvement. Portfolios can help propel you into a thoughtful, rigorous, and thorough process of self-reflection, which, perhaps, is one of the greatest potential benefits to their use.

Reflection is another way of saying self-evaluation. Having teachers self-evaluate provides the opportunity to continually improve and to sustain success in our profession. When teachers think about what works well and what could work better, the likelihood that they will know how to improve , and will actually make improvements change, is dramatically increased. After all, the best evaluation we could ever hope to receive is that which we apply to ourselves.

Underlying beliefs for using portfolios as a professional-development tool include the following:

- ◆ Teachers need to assess their own practice.

- ◆ Teachers need personalized professional learning opportunities.

- ◆ Teachers want to improve their practice and knowledge.

- ◆ Teachers are capable of assuming responsibility for a significant portion of their own professional growth.[8]

Self-reflection can be part of the professional development process through written comments the teacher adds to artifacts in the portfolio, written analyses drawn from videos of teaching episodes, descriptions of teaching philosophy and beliefs, as well as other techniques for reflecting upon one's work. However, a note of caution is in order as you consider what artifacts to select and how to use them in a thoughtful, reflective portfolio. As one writer noted: "Far too many teachers spend valuable time putting photos, certificates, and lesson plans into elaborate scrapbooks that they mistakenly refer to as portfolios. …Thoughtful reflection, not a color printer, is the key to portfolio success."[9]

Portfolios and Collaboration

"Collaboration enriches professional growth and development"[10] and the portfolio is an excellent vehicle for facilitating collaboration. Because portfolios can reflect the traditionally "invisible" aspects of teaching, such as planning, written feedback to students, communications with parents, and involvement in professional organizations, they provide supervisors with a far richer sampling of your work than mere observation would offer. You, as the teacher, become an equal partner in shaping the discussion about what you do as a teacher, and the portfolio becomes a means of communicating with others about what you value and how you are serving children. Supervisors are better able to understand who you are as a professional and can more easily engage in meaningful dialogue about your work with students, parents, and colleagues. In addition, supervisory conferences can become more substantive when they are based on examples of lesson plans and student work samples that provide a running record of instruction over time.

Just as the portfolio can provide a more in-depth portrayal of your instruction for discussion with supervisors, it also can be the subject of conversations with peers. Teachers can work together to develop their portfolios, offering suggestions for improvement in the content or presentation of material. Because the depth and breadth of your units of study are more apparent when they are presented as a whole in the portfolio, teachers can use portfolios to share ideas with other faculty members, especially new teachers. Teachers can use the portfolio material to discuss instructional issues regarding pacing, technology, and assessments. Thus, portfolios can be a tool not only for self-reflection but also for reflection from others on improvement and professional development.

Summary

A quality teaching portfolio, whether it's designed primarily for evaluation, professional development, or both, tends to reflect these key features:

- It rests squarely on sound professional teaching standards (i.e., job responsibilities).

- It contains purposefully selected artifacts of both student and teacher work, which accurately document the teacher's major job responsibilities.

- It includes thoughtful commentary about *what* the artifacts included in the portfolio mean and *how* the teacher learned from their use (reflection).[11]

Teaching portfolios have become popular largely because of their flexible nature and practical value to teachers. They can be used for a range of activities including pre-service training, hiring, certification, and career advancement. Most importantly, they elevate teachers as professionals and give them a role in their own development and evaluation. As you read through this book and consider your own design, development, and use of teacher portfolios, we hope that we confirm your own experiences with portfolios or pique your interest regarding the possibilities of professional portfolios for teachers.

A Case Study: National Board for Professional Teaching Standards[12]

One of the most persuasive examples of the portfolio as a tool for professionalizing teaching is the National Board certification process. The National Board for Professional Teaching Standards (NBPTS) was founded in 1987 and has certified nearly 10,000 teachers in 20 different specialty areas in the intervening years. Two of their primary functions have been to establish standards for teaching in certificate fields and to provide a voluntary assessment process for National Board certification.[13] Ideally, the broader vision of the role for the Board is to "encourage the development of highly qualified teachers and advance the status of the teaching profession."[14] The centerpiece of the certification process is the development of a portfolio, which provides the framework for examining a candidate's teaching and its impact on student learning. The portfolio for each teacher is organized around the competencies identified by his or her home state, but the ultimate focal point is effective teaching practices.

Although evaluative in nature, the certification assessment is sufficiently rigorous and detailed in its analysis of a teacher's work that it offers insights on even the most capable teacher's instruction.

According to research on teachers who have undergone the assessment process, "the certification process, especially the creation of the portfolio [is] a powerful and transforming professional development experience."[15] The certification process has been not only a process for professional recognition of the teachers' skills and knowledge but one in which they have developed a deeper and more analytical understanding of instruction. Teacher candidates identified the following benefits of the certification process:

- greater professional confidence

- improved analysis of instruction

- clearer focus on student outcomes

- greater commitment to professional growth.[16]

In addition to these important professional advantages, there is broad political support for National Board certification. Twenty-five states now have state licensure incentives for earning National Board certification and 31 states offer financial incentives.[17]

A recent validity study of the National Board certification process found that the teachers who were Board certified:

- Possess pedagogical content knowledge that is more flexibly and innovatively employed in instruction.

- Are more able to improvise and to alter instruction in response to contextual features of the classroom situation.

- Understand at a deeper level the reasons for individual student success and failure on any given academic task.

- Are more able to provide developmentally appropriate learning tasks that engage, challenge, and even intrigue students.

- Are more able to anticipate and plan for difficulties students are likely to encounter with new concepts.

- Can more easily improvise when things do not run smoothly.

- Are more able to generate accurate hypotheses about the causes of student success and failure.

- Bring a distinct passion to their work.[18]

A Case Study: Connecticut's Beginning Educator Support and Training Program (BEST)

At the state level, Connecticut has established a model program that other states are beginning to emulate. Its program is referred to as BEST, Beginning Educator Support and Training Program, and an important component of the program is the development of a teaching portfolio. Currently, Connecticut and New York are the only states in the country that have state performance assessment programs, versus paper and pencil tests, to determine eligibility for the second stage of teacher certification (three years after initial license), and Connecticut has the distinction of being the only state that uses portfolios as part of the process. Kentucky requires a portfolio and a videotaped lesson as part of the evaluation process for beginning teachers to earn their initial professional certificates.[19] Three additional states (Arizona, Indiana, and North Carolina) are considering the use of portfolios in their assessments of new teachers.[20]

BEST requires that local school districts provide new teachers with a mentor, at least during their first year of teaching. During the second year, teachers must develop a portfolio with written summaries and reflections on their teaching that explore not only what they did in particular lessons but what they would do differently in the future. They also submit videotapes of their teaching. Trained, experienced teachers review the portfolios, and, if the new teacher does not receive a 2 on a scale of 1 to 4, he or she is given one additional opportunity during the third year to redo the portfolio and videotape. Those who receive a 2 or better receive provisional licensure, and those who do not are denied a license. Although state officials point out that the objective of the portfolio and videotape assessment is to improve the quality of teaching in Connecticut not to fail more teachers, the number of teachers denied licenses has increased, suggesting a more rigorous process. The portfolios were intended to emphasize "aspects of good teaching, such as continual reflection and the adjustment of instruction to meet the needs of students with different learning styles."[21]

BEST is a recent addition to an evolving educational policy in Connecticut, termed "The Balanced Equation" that began in the early 1980s. Similar to efforts in other states, heightened expectations for teachers were paired with increased support and compensation. Significant progress has been made in providing improved compensation as evidenced by the fact that Connecticut has the fifth highest teacher salaries in the country when adjusted for the cost of living. BEST is just one of multiple policy initiatives intended to enhance the teacher quality side of "The Balanced Equation."

Case Study: The Douglas County Outstanding Teacher Program[22]

The Douglas County (Colorado) Outstanding Teacher Program offers an example of how portfolios can be used at the local level for a pay-for-performance plan. With expertise from one of the early research efforts using portfolios at Stanford University, Douglas County was able to develop this program through a joint effort by the school system, teacher union, Board of Education, and community members.

According to the Outstanding Teacher Program, compensation for individual teachers is based on general pay, responsibility pay, and group incentives. General pay constitutes the most significant portion of teacher compensation and is composed of:

- base pay
- education credit
- evaluation credit
- skill development bonuses
- master teacher increases.

For the "evaluation credit," teachers are assessed using the standard evaluation process in the county and are judged "proficient" or "unsatisfactory." If they are found "proficient," they receive the annual salary raise.

To be found "outstanding" and receive the $1000 skill development bonus, teachers must submit a professional portfolio to document their practice. An administrator at the same school assesses the portfolio and determines whether the teacher is outstanding based on the program's assessment criteria. The assessment criteria clearly define the competencies for an outstanding educator and are organized around the three major categories of (a) assessment and instruction, (b) content and pedagogy, and (c) collaboration and partnership. The required elements of the portfolio are:

- résumé
- philosophy of education statement
- commentary for the three major categories
- six artifacts accompanied by a rationale and representing the three categories
- reflection based on client and peer surveys
- recent evaluation or growth plan
- a self-evaluation.[23]

During the first year of implementation, 32 percent of the eligible teachers submitted portfolios and 90 percent of them were awarded the "outstanding" designation. The pay-for-performance program was considered a success on a number of levels, but the most tangible support was shown by a 96 percent vote of support by the teachers to ratify the district contract that included it. It is considered to have wide political support.

Based on this pay-for-performance plan, teachers are compensated differentially for individual performance at multiple levels. Most important, however, "the purpose of this program is to reward highly effective teachers and promote the professional development of all teachers who participate in the program, with the ultimate aim of advancing student learning."[24] The impact on the professional development of teachers and student learning remain to be documented, but the portfolio is viewed as a viable vehicle for pursuing these goals.

References

1. Tchudi, S. N., & Huerta, M. C. (1983). *Teaching writing in the content areas: Middle school/junior high.* Washington, DC: National Education Association.

2. Wolf, K., Lichtenstein, G., & Stevenson, C. (1997). Portfolios in teacher evaluation. In J. H. Stronge (Ed.), *Evaluating teaching: A guide to current thinking and best practice* (pp. 193–214). Thousand Oaks, CA: Corwin Press, Inc., p. 194.

3. Doolittle, P. (1994). *Teacher portfolio assessment.* ERIC/AE Digest. Washington, DC: ERIC Clearinghouse on Assessment and Evaluation: The Catholic University of America, Department of Education, p. 1.

4. Oakley, K. (1998). The performance assessment system: A portfolio assessment model for evaluating beginning teachers. *Journal of Personnel Evaluation in Education, 11,* 323–341, p. 323.

5. Shulman, L. S. (1988). A union of insufficiencies: Strategies for teacher assessment in a period of reform. *Educational Leadership, 46*(3), 36–41.

6. Wolf, K., Lichtenstein, G., & Stevenson, C. (1997), p. 194.

7. Portions of this section are adapted from Helm, V. M., & Stronge, J. H. (1994). *Using multiple data sources: The key to effective performance evaluation in education.* Unpublished manuscript.

8. See, for example, Airasian, P. W., & Gullickson, A. (1997). Teacher self-evaluation. In J. H. Stronge (Ed.), *Evaluating teaching: A guide to current thinking and best practice* (pp. 215–247). Thousand Oaks, CA: Corwin Press; Osterman, K. F., & Kottkamp, R. B. (1993). *Reflective practice for educators: Im-*

proving schooling through professional development. Newbury Park, CA: Corwin Press.

9. Painter, B. (2001). Using teaching portfolios. *Educational Leadership, 58*(5), 31–34, p. 32.

10. Airasian, P. W., & Gullickson, A. (1997), p. 216.

11. Wolf, K., Lichtenstein, G., & Stevenson, C. (1997), p. 195.

12. Pearlman, M. (1997, March). *Designing in validity: The National Board for Professional Teaching Standards certification assessments.* Paper presented at the annual conference of the American Educational Research Association, Chicago, IL.

13. Harman, A. E. (2001). A wider role for the National Board. *Educational Leadership, 58*(8), 54–55.

14. Bohen, D. B. (2001). Strengthening teachers through national certification. *Educational Leadership, 58*(8), 50–53, p. 50.

15. Bohen, D. B. (2001), p. 50.

16. Bohen, D. B. (2001).

17. Jerald, C. D. (2000). The state of the states. In V.B. Edwards (Ed.), Quality counts 2000: Who should teach? *Education Week, XIX*(18), 62–67.

18. Bond, L., Smith, T., Baker, W. K., & Hattie, J. A. (2000). *The certification system of the National Board for Professional Teaching Standards: A construct and consequential validity study.* Greensboro, NC: Center for Educational Research and Evaluation, The University of North Carolina at Greensboro, p. 140.

19. Jerald, C. D., & Boser, U. (2000). Setting policies for new teachers. In V. B. Edwards (Ed.), Quality Counts 2000: Who should teach? *Education Week, XIX*(18), 44–47.

20. Archer, J. (2000). Earning their stripes. In V.B. Edwards (Ed.), Quality Counts 2000: Who should teach? *Education Week, XIX*(18), 38–43.

21. Archer, J. (2000), p. 43.

22. Wolf, K., Lichtenstein, G., Bartlett, E., & Hartman, D. (1996). Professional development and teaching portfolios: The Douglas County Outstanding Teacher Program. *Journal of Personnel Evaluation in Education, 10*(3), 279–286.

23. Wolf, K., Lichtenstein, G., Bartlett, E., & Hartman, D. (1996), p. 282.

24. Wolf, K., Lichtenstein, G., Bartlett, E., & Hartman, D. (1996), p. 280.

2

DEVELOPING A TEACHER PORTFOLIO

True wisdom is to know what is best worth knowing,
and to do what is best worth doing.
Edward Porter Humprey

The image of a professional artist carrying a large, bound *portfolio* of her work is familiar enough to us, and it is an image that readily comes to mind when one mentions portfolios. But what image comes to mind when one speaks of teacher portfolios? How should teachers present collections of artifacts intended to capture the essence and quality of their performance as planners, instructors, assessors, classroom managers, and as contributing members of the profession? We suggest that effective portfolios are deliberately structured to allow for both accountability and creativity. There are, therefore, some very practical questions to consider when developing teacher portfolios. In this chapter, we answer several of those key questions both for teachers and for administrators who may be responsible for developing a portfolio program:

- ◆ What is the role of performance standards in developing portfolios?
- ◆ What should a portfolio "look like"?
- ◆ What is the role of artifacts in portfolios?
- ◆ How can captions add value to portfolios?

What is the Role of Performance Standards in Developing Portfolios?

In Chapter 1, we make the case that in order to have a basis for documenting and evaluating performance, you must first define *what* teachers should know and be able to do. That is the role of performance standards in a portfolio-based evaluation system. The portfolio, then, is a means of accounting for a teacher's development within the context of that set of professional performance standards.

15

But teaching is a highly integrated craft, so how does one define teaching in terms of performance standards? Perhaps, in part, due to the standards movement in K–12 schools, there is a proliferation of sources for identifying professional performance standards. Call them performance standards, job responsibilities, critical competencies, or a host of other names, but they remain a set of identified skills vital to effective teaching.

Sources abound. The National Board for Professional Teaching Standards (NBPTS) has developed criteria identifying key teacher responsibilities for teachers seeking national certification.[1] The Interstate Teacher Assessment and Support Consortium (INTASC) has developed a model for principles of effective teaching.[2] The Performance Assessment System (PAS), developed as a consortium of urban and rural school districts in California, Washington state, Maryland, and North Carolina, uses a combination of NBPTS, INTASC, and state standards for its framework.[3] Connecticut serves as just one example of a state that has defined various "dimensions of teaching," which it uses in the assessment of novice teacher preparedness.[4] In a neighboring New England state, the University of Southern Maine has identified teacher performance assessment standards[5]. On the West Coast, Stanford University experimented in the early 1990s with its BioTAP program, outlining four critical areas of teaching.[6] In each of these examples, teacher responsibilities have been identified as a foundation for assessing and improving teacher performance.

Figure 2.1 (pp. 17–18) offers a comparison of teacher responsibilities among several of the sources cited above and others. These sources can serve as a helpful source to schools or districts intent upon identifying key teacher responsibilities as the foundation for their own portfolio systems.

The content of Figure 2.1 is by no means exhaustive, but it illustrates the breadth of evaluation systems and the consensus that exists among them with respect to identified teacher performance standards. Not coincidentally, each of these organizations is also an example of the use of portfolios in teacher assessment. By linking assessment directly to responsibilities of the profession, portfolios can serve as an excellent way to gauge teacher effectiveness.

Performance standards are the foundation of effective teacher evaluation systems. A fair and comprehensive evaluation system should provide sufficient detail and accuracy so that educators and their supervisors can reasonably understand their performance expectations. The expectations of teacher performance can be usefully conceptualized using a three-tiered system, in which *teaching domains* represent areas of teacher competencies, *performance standards* are the competencies that teachers are expected to exhibit, and *performance indicators* are specific examples of those competencies. Figure 2.2 (p. 19) illustrates the hierarchical relationship among these three levels of description.

Figure 2.1. Examples of Articulated Teacher Responsibilities

National Board for Professional Teaching Standards[7]	Interstate New Teacher Assessment and Support Consortium[8]	Performance Assessment System[9]	University of Southern Maine[10]	Perkins & Gelfer[11]
◆ Subject area knowledge and pedagogy	◆ Structure of the disciplines	◆ Curriculum	◆ Subject-area knowledge	◆ Planning
◆ Commitment to students and learning	◆ Subject-area knowledge	◆ Instruction	◆ Child-centeredness	◆ Content and curriculum coverage
◆ Management and monitoring of student learning	◆ How children learn and develop	◆ Resources	◆ Plans instruction	◆ Methodology and classroom organization
◆ Membership in learning communities	◆ Diverse learners	◆ Assessment	◆ Use of a variety of teaching strategies	◆ Use of appropriate resources
◆ Professional reflection and development	◆ Variety of instructional strategies	◆ Classroom environment	◆ Respect for individual differences	◆ Evaluation of student performance
	◆ MotivationAssessment	◆ Professionalism	◆ Student assessment	◆ Management of classroom instruction and behavior
	◆ Communication		◆ Classroom management	◆ Communication
	◆ Relationships		◆ Promotes principles of democratic citizenship	◆ Professionalism
	◆ Professional growth		◆ Communication	
			◆ Professional inquiry	
			◆ Professional responsibility/service	

Figure continues on next page.

Connecticut Department of Education[12]	Williamsburg-James City County Public Schools[13]	Wheeler[14]	BioTAP[15]	Howard & McClosky[16]
◆ Content knowledge ◆ Content pedagogy ◆ Learner-centeredness ◆ Professional responsibility	◆ Planning for and delivering instruction ◆ Assessing student performance ◆ Managing the learning environment ◆ Professionalism	◆ Knowledge of subject matter ◆ Instructional competence ◆ Assessment competence ◆ Other duties to the school and community ◆ Professionalism	◆ Planning and preparation ◆ Instruction ◆ Evaluation and reflection ◆ Professional growth and service	◆ Planning ◆ Instruction ◆ Assessment ◆ Teacher impact ◆ Student motivation and management ◆ Professional growth and contributions

---

Figure 2.2. Expectations of Teacher Performance

Teaching Domains

Performance Standards

Performance Indicators

For purposes of this text and for the examples provided in it, we have identified four *Teaching Domains:*

1. Instructional Skills

2. Assessment Skills

3. Learning Environment Skills

4. Professionalism

Within each domain, *performance standards* describe the actual duties and activities in which teachers engage. For example, an important instructional skill is to select and use resources that are compatible with students' needs and abilities. In the area of assessment, a teacher must be able to assess student performance and use assessment results to make daily and long-range decisions. Performance standards define the domains of teaching at a functional level of specificity. In other words, performance standards put teacher responsibilities into operational terms.

Figure 2.3 illustrates how the domain of professionalism can be articulated through four specific performance standards. Certainly, individuals or organizations may debate the specific categorization or wording of these performance standards, but the figure offers one possible iteration.

**Figure 2.3. Sample Performance Standards
for the Teacher Domain of Professionalism**

Domain: Professionalism

♦ The teacher demonstrates ethical and professional behavior.

♦ The teacher participates in an on-going process of professional development.

♦ The teacher contributes to the overall school climate by supporting school goals.

♦ The teacher initiates and maintains timely communication with parents/guardians and administrators concerning student progress or problems.

Beyond the level of performance standards, *performance indicators* provide an even greater level of specificity for teacher responsibilities. Performance indicators are used in an evaluation system to do just what the term implies: They indicate a teacher's performance in terms of observable behaviors. However, any list of performance indicators is not intended to be exhaustive, nor are such indicators meant to be prescriptive. Instead, performance indicators serve as examples of specific behaviors that are illustrative of the standards. Figure 2.4 illustrates sample performance indicators for the fourth performance standard under "Professionalism," which was listed in the previous figure.

Figure 2.4. Sample Performance Indicators

Domain: Professionalism

Performance Standard: The teacher initiates and maintains timely communications with parents/guardians and administrators concerning student progress or problems.

♦ The teacher responds promptly to parental concerns.

♦ The teacher encourages parental involvement within the school.

♦ The teacher provides information regarding school/community functions to parents/guardians.

♦ The teacher works with community members in carrying out school and community sponsored functions.

A complete set of teacher domains, performance standards, and performance indicators has been developed to serve as a generic model for this text or for an organization seeking to develop its own framework for teacher responsibilities. Please see "Performance Standards" in Appendix A and on the companion CD for details.

Performance standards are essentially a definitional description of the craft of teaching. By identifying what a teacher should know and be able to do, you are defining a measure by which teachers can judge their own work and have their performance evaluated by others. Whether portfolios comprise an element of a given evaluation system or not, standards of performance should be central to any evaluation system. Moreover, when performance standards are tied to teacher portfolios, you have the basis for an evaluation mechanism characterized by a balance of accountability and creativity.

What Should a Teacher Portfolio "Look Like"?

In Chapter 1, we offer several definitions of a *teacher portfolio*, which, in its most fundamental form, is a structured collection of information about a teacher's performance. But what does a teacher portfolio actually *look like*? The possibilities for the form that portfolios take may be limited only by what's available at your local office supply store. From cardboard boxes to computer disks, from notebooks to boxes, portfolios can take myriad forms, depending upon contents, purposes, and needs.

Yet, whatever a portfolio may "look like," there are certain features that all types of professional teacher portfolios should have in common. We see four essential features for effective teacher portfolios. They must (a) provide organization, (b) be portable, (c) accommodate typical artifacts of teaching, and (d) be flexible enough to accommodate change over time. Figure 2.5 (p. 22) explores these four features.

Portfolio Notebook

As mentioned earlier, there are any number of possible forms that a portfolio may take: envelopes, file folders, expandable files, boxes, and canvas bags, for example. Our decided preference is the *portfolio notebook*. Our experience in working with schools and school districts in the development of portfolios has led us again and again to the selection of a standard three-ring notebook with tabbed sections as a simple, easy-to-use, and affordable format. Using tabbed dividers is a simple means of organizing the portfolio notebook. Four tabs can identify four domains of teaching, and documents within each section can be further organized by specific responsibility. Notebooks, of course, are readily portable. In several schools and districts, we have seen a standard one-inch notebook adopted as the accepted format of teacher portfolios, with the proviso that if an item cannot fit in the portfolio notebook then it should not be included. This ensures portability and it helps to reduce the steamer-trunk mentality of collecting items indiscriminately. The portfolio notebook is designed specifically to hold multiple pages of paper, which we have found to be the most typical medium for artifacts of teaching. Finally, the portfolio notebook accommodates change over time, enabling outdated and outmoded documents to be removed and new ones inserted, thereby giving evidence of professional growth. Throughout this text, the portfolio notebook will be used as the basis for our model.

Figure 2.5. Four Essential Physical Features of Teacher Portfolios

No matter what the form of portfolios they must…	provide *organization…*	*so that…*	◆ defined performance standards can be documented explicitly. ◆ there is consistency among portfolios and, therefore, a common, reliable basis upon which to evaluate performance.
	be *portable…*		◆ teachers may work on them in multiple settings. ◆ teachers may readily share them with colleagues and supervisors. ◆ supervisors may review them in multiple settings.
	accommodate *typical artifacts* of teaching…		◆ the types of artifacts that most commonly document teaching competencies are easily contained within the portfolio.
	be flexible enough to accommodate *change over time…*		◆ professional growth can be made evident with the removal of outmoded/out-dated artifacts and the inclusion of new ones.

Digital Portfolio

It bears mentioning that one notable version of the portfolio notebook is the digital portfolio. As with all things technological, the application of current hardware and software to the development and implementation of a portfolio system of teacher supervision is evolving. Thus, there are some immediate possibilities for the use of digital portfolios. Whether through the use of computer diskettes, CD-ROMs, or local area networks, digital portfolios can offer a school or school district a practical avenue for a teacher portfolio system. But, there are limitations as well. Figure 2.6 indicates the advantages and disadvantages of digital portfolios.

Figure 2.6. Advantages and Disadvantages of Digital Portfolios[17]

Advantages	*Disadvantages*
◆ Easy transfer of information among portfolio creators, colleagues, and reviewers	◆ Requires specific hardware (e.g., personal work stations, multimedia work station, etc.)
◆ Storage and display of multiple data formats, including text, graphics, sound, pictures, and video	◆ Requires specific software (e.g., word processing, multimedia, etc.)
◆ Universal template can be created to provide structure and consistency among portfolios	◆ Start-up costs may be prohibitive
◆ Reduced paper and space needs	◆ Requires technological training for portfolio creators and reviewers

---

From hard copy formats to digitized ones, portfolios are intended to provide an avenue for teachers to demonstrate and improve their professional performance. What should become evident throughout this text is that scrapbooks and steamer trunks—even the artist's portfolio—are not conducive to meaningful teacher portfolios.[18] Although we advocate a notebook format, deciding on the specific format of portfolios in a given school or school district depends upon a combination of the organization's resources, purposes, and needs.

Portfolios for Other Purposes: Action Research Portfolios and Employment Portfolios

A photographer's portfolio is intended to illustrate the breadth and quality of his or her work. A captain's log is a kind of portfolio, intended to document continuous performance. A committee's minutes of meetings are intended to capture the process and decisions of its work. Each of these "portfolios" has a different purpose. A teacher's portfolio, as we define it in this text, is designed to promote professional growth and accountability, both through the portfolio development process itself and through the review of the portfolio by another professional. However, depending on the setting and particular needs of an individual, school, or educational organization, teacher portfolios may have other purposes and formats. The action research portfolio and the employment portfolio are two such examples.

The *action research portfolio* aims to implement, evaluate, and improve instructional practices at the classroom or school level. In an action research portfolio, a teacher identifies an area or areas within his or her professional practice that he or she wishes to understand better and to improve. The structure of the portfolio then becomes determined by the teacher's collection of evidence to address his or her action research questions. For example, a teacher may want to determine whether the use of manipulatives increases students' mastery of adding and subtracting fractions compared to using paper-and-pencil problems alone. The teacher may compare two or more of his or her current classes, or compare this year's students to last year's. However the teacher decides to address the action research question, the portfolio becomes the means for structuring the study and documenting the results.

The action research portfolio becomes even more powerful, though, when it is not limited to an individual teacher addressing a single question in isolation. Action research portfolios can require collaboration among horizontal or vertical teams of teachers to address multiple strands of broad questions. For instance, a middle school faculty may ask, "How do we most efficiently move students from a basic understanding of fractions at the beginning of the 6th grade to mastery of algebraic equations at the end of the 8th?" The content and skill strands that feed into this question are divided among faculty members to pursue through action research, and the portfolio then becomes the means of answering the research question and sharing results among faculty members.

The *employment portfolio* is another example of a portfolio designed for purposes other than accountability and professional growth. Portfolios are becoming increasingly common—even expected—in teacher job interviews. The employment portfolio is a collection of artifacts that illustrate a teacher candidate's knowledge and skills as a professional. A novice teacher may develop such a portfolio when seeking his or her first position; therefore, the portfolio highlights the teacher's educational background and student teaching experiences. It may be organized by competencies developed or by experiences in a preparation program.

Similarly, a veteran teacher may develop an employment portfolio to illustrate her background, skills, and range of experiences over the course of her career. The veteran teacher also may wish to structure the employment portfolio around competencies, in which case the portfolio notebook designed around performance standards that we advocate would be an excellent model! Indeed, we have recommended to the schools and districts with whom we have worked that their teachers' portfolios always be considered the teachers' property. For teachers, this means that their portfolio can, in fact, serve as an employment portfolio should they be in a position of seeking a job elsewhere. Whether for a novice or veteran teacher, an employment portfolio is intended to demonstrate to a prospective principal that a teacher candidate has the requisite knowledge and skills for the job. How such a portfolio is structured is left to the discretion of the individual teacher and reflects what that teacher views as most valuable and most important to emphasize.

What Is the Role of Artifacts in Portfolios?

The portfolio process requires teachers to be observers, to be self-critical, to conduct research, to collaborate, to allow for mistakes, and to learn continuously.[19] This complex combination of habits and skills must be used as teachers are assembling their portfolios. Teachers must grapple with the responsibilities for which they are accountable, and then they must identify the artifacts of their work that can serve as evidence of their performance. Artifacts, therefore, are central to the portfolio process.

What are Artifacts?

Artifacts are the products and by-products of teaching that demonstrate a teacher's performance. They are the raw materials on which teachers reflect and from which they learn. Figure 2.7 offers three other recent definitions that may be helpful.

Figure 2.7. Definitions of *Artifact*

Author(s)	*Definition*
Wolf[20]	"Tangible evidence of teaching and learning."
Riggs & Sandlin[21]	"Actual documents of the life and work of the teacher."
Painter[22]	"Any evidence that teachers use to document or support how they meet teaching standards."

Types of Artifacts Available to Teachers

Although the number of artifacts from which a teacher may choose is limited only by his or her creativity, every artifact can essentially be grouped by two characteristics: (1) who produced it? and (2) why was it produced? Answering these questions provides a helpful matrix by which to categorize the many artifacts that may possibly be included in a teacher portfolio. Figure 2.8 (p. 26) represents a variety of possible types of artifacts grouped by category.

Figure 2.8. Types of Artifacts Grouped by Category[23]

Produced by the Teacher About the Teacher

- Photojournal depicting classroom activities
- Photos of classroom environment
- Bibliographies of texts, resources, etc., used
- Documentation of in-service training or coursework
- Videotape of teaching
- Audio tape of teaching
- Written description about instruction
- Résumé
- Statement of philosophy of education
- Professional development plan

Produced by Others About the Teacher

- Parent surveys
- Student surveys
- Interviews
- Focus groups
- Peer observations
- Teacher competency tests (e.g., Praxis)
- Unsolicited letters/notes from parents, students, colleagues, & community members
- Solicited letters of recommendation
- Previous evaluations by supervisors
- Awards or recognition
- Newspaper articles about the teacher

Produced by the Teacher for Teaching

- Teacher-made assessments (e.g., tests, quizzes, rubrics, etc.)
- Assessment feedback to students
- Learning styles inventory
- Case studies of students
- Action research results
- Professional articles or presentations by teacher
- Lesson plans
- Modifications of lesson plans
- Computer-generated presentation materials
- Classroom management plan
- Samples of communication with parents and students
- Unit overviews
- Pupil gain data
- Teacher-made instructional materials (e.g., handouts)

Produced by Others for Learning

- Student assessment results (i.e., student performance on assessments, including standardized tests, teacher-made tests, projects, etc.)
- Student work samples (i.e., student performance on instructional activities and assignments)

Although there are 39 examples of artifacts listed in Figure 2.8, these examples are not intended to be exhaustive. Teaching is a creative, ever-evolving craft. Therefore, one would expect that other examples of meaningful artifacts will continue to emerge or may already be obvious to you from your own experience. Also, there is a level of specificity not addressed in the lists above. For example, under "Samples of communications with parents," a teacher might include class newsletters, a log of telephone contacts, samples of progress reports, records of parent–teacher conferences, and more.

Our contention, in short, is that the very act of teaching lends itself to documentation through artifacts. Indeed, they meet three important criteria for useful artifacts:

1. Each of the artifacts listed in Figure 2.8 is a product or by-product of teaching. In other words, these artifacts would not be created solely for inclusion in a portfolio.

2. Each of the artifacts can be readily reviewed in a portfolio form. Indeed, of the 39 artifacts listed, only four are not inherently conducive to being included in a portfolio notebook. However, we have advised districts that choose notebooks as their portfolio format to allow for teachers and administrators to prearrange for nonstandard artifact entries, such as videotapes, when appropriate.

3. They all are evidentiary of one or more of the performance standards that we have identified previously in our model of teaching competencies in this chapter. To illustrate this point, lists of artifacts cross-referenced with illustrative performance standards are found in the appendices.

How Can Captions Add Value to Portfolios?

Artifacts are evidence of teaching, but it must be recognized that an artifact in a portfolio is clearly out of the context in which it was intended to be used. For this reason, a caption should accompany each artifact. A *caption* is simply a notation, or series of notations, attached to an artifact to guide the reviewer's understanding of the artifact. Each artifact should include certain information, as shown in Figure 2.9.

Figure 2.9. Contents of a Caption[24]

Each Caption Should Include...

- Descriptive title of the artifact

- Performance standard documented by the artifact

- Date created

- Who created the artifact

- Brief description of context in which the artifact was used

- Additional commentary by the teacher (if desired)

Captions should be brief and descriptive, much like a road sign is for a driver. Indeed, captions can serve as "road signs" for a reviewer as he or she navigates through a teacher's portfolio. But what should these road signs look like? There are several possibilities. A school or school district may wish to standardize a procedure for creating captions. The example below illustrates one possible format designed for itemizing the contents of each section of a portfolio. The teacher completes a series of forms for the artifacts in his or her portfolio, places the forms at the beginning of the corresponding sections of his or her portfolio, and the list serves as a table of contents for the reviewer.

Figure 2.10. Sample Standardized Caption

Artifact # _____

Description of Artifact:

Responsibility Documented:

Context and Date Used:

Teacher Comment (optional):

Another strategy for employing captions is to affix captions to each individual artifact so that the caption can be readily reviewed with the artifact. Again, a school or school district may standardize a format and provide the actual forms to teachers for their use in assembling their portfolios. In this case, a caption form may be approximately the size of a note card and could be stapled or clipped to the artifact. Portfolio artifacts also can be placed in clear plastic sheaths within a notebook, in which case the caption card can simply be slid into the sheath with the artifact.

Captions can also be provided in less formal ways. An effective method is to provide brief descriptions of artifacts typed on standard paper and then trimmed down to attach to or include with artifacts. Figure 2.11 illustrates a teacher-made caption for an artifact. Sticky notes are an inexpensive and easy-to-use medium, as well. In any case, we suggest that the essential content of a helpful caption—as listed in Figure 2.10—be included to guide the reader's review of the portfolio. As one observer noted a decade ago, "Documents without captions are meaningless."[25]

Figure 2.11. Sample Teacher-Made Caption

I-3   *Instructional Skills. Attached is a lesson plan that incorporates the five National Foreign Language Standards. It is designed to complement a textbook unit on Paris. It gives students the opportunity to express themselves using four types of communication in French (reading, writing, listening and speaking).*

How Can Portfolios be Organized Effectively?

Rather than just providing a snapshot, a teacher portfolio is intended to demonstrate a teacher's professional growth over time. A portfolio is intended to illuminate the context in which a teacher teaches in order to help evaluate performance. A portfolio is also a means of capturing the quality of a teacher's performance. But time, context, and quality all change. Given these aims of portfolio design, it is evident that portfolios must be fluid in nature.

A teacher's portfolio changes as his or her skills, abilities, knowledge, practice, and achievement change. In this sense, a portfolio is a "living document."[26] Because of this fluidity, the organization of a teacher's portfolio is extremely important. It is the organization, after all, that provides structure and continuity to a series of artifacts and captions that are subject to ongoing change and revision. Moreover, when portfolios are used for high-stakes purposes, such as teacher evaluation, it is incumbent upon the school or school district to design a review system that is accurate, fair, useful, and feasible.[27]

How can teacher portfolios be organized most effectively? When portfolios are used for professional growth and teacher evaluation, there are several valid strategies for their organization. We explore two fundamental means here:

(a) Organization around performance standards, and (b) organization around specific, required artifacts that are linked to performance standards.

Using Performance Standards to Organize Portfolios

Earlier in this chapter, we make the case that defining expectations or standards for teachers' performance is essential to developing portfolios. Again, we offer a conceptual model for capturing the domains of responsibility for teachers as four distinct areas, illustrated in Figure 2.12. (Please see "Performance Standards" in Appendix A for a complete description of each of these domains, defined as specific performance standards.)

Figure 2.12. Domains of Teacher Performance Standards

Instructional Skills

Assessment Skills

Learning Environment Skills

Professionalism

Using a school's or district's articulated standards of performance for teachers is a simple and logical organizer for teacher portfolios. For example, referring to the four domains of teaching identified in Figure 2.12, teacher portfolios would be organized into four distinct sections, one section for each domain. Then the specific performance standards that comprise each of these four areas would constitute subsets of the organization of the portfolios. An individual teacher who is assembling his or her portfolio would then select artifacts that document each of the performance standards for which he or she is accountable.

As we advocate them, teacher portfolios are essentially built upon the interrelationship between teacher responsibilities and the artifacts that provide evidence that those responsibilities are being met. Figure 2.13 illustrates this idea.

Figure 2.13 includes just four examples of possible teacher standards and how various artifacts could be selected to document those standards. The complete model in the appendices includes a total of 18 performance standards. Therefore, a teacher portfolio in a school that employs this particular model could be organized into four sections and 18 subsections.

Figure 2.13. The Interrelationship Between Performance Standards and Artifacts

Sample Performance Standards	*Sample Artifacts*
The teacher demonstrates current and accurate knowledge of subject matter covered in the curriculum.	◆ Course syllabus ◆ Unit lesson plans ◆ List of in-service activities
The teacher provides a variety of on-going and culminating assessments to measure student performance.	◆ Teacher-made tests or quizzes ◆ Explanation of grading procedures ◆ Sample of grade recording system
The teacher communicates clear expectations about behavior to students and parents.	◆ Explanation of classroom management procedures ◆ Teacher-student communications
The teacher participates in an ongoing process of professional development.	◆ List of in-service activities ◆ Example of a product created from a professional development activity

---

The Dallas Public Schools (DPS) provide another example of how performance standards may be used to organize teacher portfolios.[28] In the DPS model of teaching, there are five domains. Figure 2.14 (p. 32) illustrates these domains and several sample artifacts that teachers might select to document their performance in these areas.

Regardless of how the craft of teaching may be conceptualized, the use of specifically defined performance standards as an organizer for teacher portfolios is valid. Simply put, the expectations for teachers are articulated, and individual teachers document that they are meeting these expectations by providing artifacts and captions that illustrate how the expectations are being met. Organizing teacher portfolios around performance standards provides the structure necessary for a system of evaluation and professional growth. However, it also provides teachers sufficient latitude to use their professional judgement and discretion in selecting the artifacts that they believe will best illustrate the quality of their performance.[29]

**Figure 2.14. Dallas Public Schools
Teacher Domains and Sample Artifacts**

Teacher Domain	*Sample Artifacts*
Knowledge of Subject Matter	◆ Content workshops attended ◆ Tests of content knowledge ◆ Academic degrees earned
Planning and Organizing for Instruction	◆ Curriculum map ◆ Sample lesson plan ◆ Student work samples
Assessment Skills	◆ Sample feedback ◆ Teacher-made tests ◆ Copy of grading policy
Professionalism and Communication	◆ Organizational memberships ◆ Presentations ◆ Publications
School and Community Service	◆ Committee memberships ◆ Sponsorships ◆ Outreach activities

---

Using Required Entries to Organize Portfolios

An alternative to organizing portfolios around performance standards alone is to define a portfolio around specific, required artifacts that are linked to performance standards. As an organizer, this method reduces teacher discretion in selecting artifacts; however, it increases the consistency of content among teacher portfolios.

One model suggests organizing teacher portfolios into three sections:

1. Background information
2. Teaching artifacts and reflections
3. Professional information.

Within each of these three sections of a teacher's portfolio, certain artifacts are then required, as Figure 2.15 illustrates.

Figure 2.15. A Model for Organizing Teacher Portfolios Around Required Artifacts[30]

Organizing Area	*Required Artifacts*
Background Information	♦ Résumé
	♦ Background information on teacher and teaching context
	♦ Educational philosophy and teaching goals
Teaching Artifacts and Reflections	♦ Documentation of an extended teaching activity
	♦ Overview of unit goals and instruction
	♦ List of resources used in unit
	♦ Two consecutive lesson plans
	♦ Student work samples
	♦ Evaluation of student work
	♦ Reflective commentary by teacher
	♦ Additional units/lessons/student work
Professional Information	♦ List of professional activities
	♦ Letters of recommendation
	♦ Formal evaluations

Other similar models abound, each of which prescribes certain artifacts that are to comprise a teacher's portfolio. The National Board for Professional Teaching Standards (NBPTS) and the Performance Assessment System (PAS) used by Teach for America are two notable examples. The NBPTS is well-regarded for its identification of rigorous competencies required for National Board certification. The artifacts required of the NBTPS in its portfolio are grounded in these competencies and, by prescribing the artifacts required of National Board candidates, the guesswork of selecting artifacts has been minimized. One result is that the focus of portfolio review is less on what artifacts were selected and more on the quality of those artifacts.

The NBPTS requires the following:

♦ Vita

♦ Written account of two selected areas

♦ Letters of support from colleagues

♦ Written description of three classes, selected by the teacher

♦ Written account of teaching and learning for a specified time or unit.[31]

The Professional Assessment System requires an even more extensive list of artifacts as the components of its teacher portfolios:

♦ Compilation of student goals for the year

♦ Report of teaching philosophy and practice

♦ Assessment of students' progress toward goals (six students total, including three selected by the teacher and three randomly selected)

♦ Lesson plans for one week with all supporting documents

♦ Videotape of classroom instruction

♦ Written evaluation by an administrator

♦ Written evaluation by a colleague

♦ Anonymous parent evaluations

♦ Anonymous student evaluations.[32]

Notably, the PAS portfolio includes other sources of data for teacher evaluation, including a videotape of instruction (which is an extension of the classic classroom observation), evaluation by a colleague (i.e., peer observation), and evaluations by parents and students. As we have stated before, the use of multiple data sources in teacher evaluation results in a more powerful model of supervision. Regarding the organization of teacher portfolios, though, the PAS is indicative of a more prescriptive model than one based on performance standards alone.

Portfolios are intended to provide a comprehensive sampling of the broad spectrum of teacher performance over time and in varying contexts. However, the portfolio, itself, is not an end; it is the means to achieving the ultimate end of improved student achievement. Organizing teacher portfolios for effectiveness and efficiency is a critical step in implementing a teacher evaluation system. Organizing portfolios requires that the role of teacher performance standards be established and that the role of artifacts relative to those standards be set. With these components in place, practical strategies for how teachers can assemble and sustain their portfolios will be addressed in the next chapter.

Summary

Developing portfolios for teacher evaluation and professional growth is a process unique to the field of education. It is a process that should be deliberate, especially with regard to documenting the specific performance standards for which teachers are held accountable and with regard to determining the appropriate format for portfolios. If teacher portfolios are to be more than mere scrapbooks of achievements, then they must exhibit both the process and the products of effective teaching. The central role of the teacher in the portfolio development process is to select the artifacts that he or she feels best demonstrate the quality and consistency of his or her performance as a teacher in the context of established performance standards. The process of creating captions for these artifacts helps to provide meaning for the reviewer, while also serving as a foundation for self-reflection, which we address in Chapter 5.

Although this chapter helps to illuminate the conceptual foundation of developing teacher portfolios, certain practical issues remain for the school or district that chooses to implement portfolios as a means of teacher evaluation and supervision. The next chapter identifies and walks through several of the practical considerations of implementing a teacher portfolio system both from the teacher's and the administrator's perspective.

References

1. National Board for Professional Teaching Standards. (1989). *Toward high and rigorous standards for the teaching profession.* Washington, DC: Author.

2. Interstate New Teacher Assessment and Support Consortium. (1992). *Model standards for beginning teacher licensing and development: A resource for state dialogue.* Washington, DC: Author.

3. Oakley, K. (1998). The Performance Assessment System: A portfolio assessment model for evaluating beginning teachers. *Journal of Personnel Evaluation in Education, 11,* 323–341.

4. Connecticut State Department of Education. (1995). *Manual for the preparation of the beginning English teacher portfolio.* Hartford, CT: Author, pp. 4–5.

5. Lyons, N. P. (1996). A grassroots experiment in performance assessment. *Educational Leadership, 53*(6), 64–67, p. 65.

6. Collins, A. (1991). Portfolios for biology teacher assessment. *Journal of Personnel Evaluation in Education, 5,* 147–167.

7. National Board for Professional Teaching Standards. (1996). *Middle childhood/generalist standards for National Board certification.* Washington, DC: Author.

8. Interstate New Teacher Assessment and Support Consortium. (1992). *Model standards for beginning teacher licensing and development: A resource for state dialogue.* Washington, DC: Author.

9. Oakley, K. (1998). The Performance Assessment System: A portfolio assessment model for evaluating beginning teachers. *Journal of Personnel Evaluation in Education, 11,* 323–341.

10. Lyons, N. P. (1996). A grassroots experiment in performance assessment. *Educational Leadership, 53*(6), 64–67.

11. Perkins, P. G., & Gelfer, J. I. (1998). Producing teacher/staff portfolios: A method for effective evaluation. *Catalyst for Change, 28*(1), 17–20.

12. Connecticut State Department of Education. (1995). *Manual for the preparation of the beginning English teacher portfolio.* Hartford, CT: Author, pp. 4–5.

13. Williamsburg-James City County Public Schools. (1996). *Teacher Evaluation System Handbook.* Williamsburg, VA: Author.

14. Wheeler, P. H. (1994). What should be included in a teacher's portfolio? *TEMP C Memo, 15*(17–20). Kalamazoo, MI: Center for Research on Educational Accountability and Teacher Evaluation.

15. Collins, A. (1991). Portfolios for biology teacher assessment. *Journal of Personnel Evaluation in Education, 5,* 147–167.

16. Howard, B. B., & McClosky, W. H. (2001). Evaluating experienced teachers. *Educational Leadership, 58*(5), 48–51.

17. Adapted from Lankes, A. D. (1995). *Electronic portfolios: A new deal in assessment.* ERIC Clearinghouse on Information and Technology (EDO–IR–95–9); Weidmer, T. L. (1998). Digital portfolios: Capturing and demonstrating skills and levels of performance. *Phi Delta Kappan, 79*(8), 586–589; and Zubizarreta, J. (1994) Teaching portfolios and the beginning teacher. *Phi Delta Kappan, 76*(3), 323–326.

18. Bird, T. (1990). The schoolteacher's portfolio: An essay on possibilities. In *The new handbook of teacher evaluation: Assessing elementary and secondary school teachers.* Newbury Park, CA: Sage.

19. Yoo, S. Y. (2001). Using portfolios to reflect on practice. *Educational Leadership, 58*(8), 78–81.

20. Wolf, K. (1999). *Leading the professional portfolio process for change.* Arlington Heights, IL: Skylight, p. 39.

21. Riggs, I. M., & Sandlin, R. A. (2000). Teaching portfolios for support of teachers' professional growth. *NASSP Bulletin, 84*(618), 22–27, p. 23.

22. Painter, B. (2001). Using teacher portfolios. *Educational Leadership, 58*(5), 31–34, p. 32.

23. See Collins, A. (1991); Curry, S. & Cruz, J. (2000). Portfolio-based teacher assessment. *Thrust for Educational Leadership, 29*(3), 34–37; Martin-Kneip, G. O. (1999). *Capturing the wisdom of practice*. Alexandria, VA: Association for Supervision and Curriculum Development, Perkins, P.G., & Gelfer, J. I. (1998). Portfolio assessment of teachers. *The ClearingHouse, 66*(4), 27–29; Peterson, K. D. (1995). *Teacher evaluation: A comprehensive guide to new directions and practices*. Thousand Oaks, CA: Corwin Press; Riggs, I. M., & Sandlin, R. A. (2000); Wolf, K. (1999); and Zubizarreta, J. (1994).

24. Wolf, K. (1994). Teaching portfolios: Capturing the complexities of teaching. In *Valuing teachers' work: New directions in teacher appraisal*. Victoria, Australia: Australian Council for Educational Research, 112–136; and Wolf, K., Lichtenstein, G., & Stevenson, C. (1997). Portfolios in teacher evaluation. In J. H. Stronge (Ed.), *Evaluating teaching: A guide to current thinking and best practice* (pp. 193–214). Thousand Oaks, CA: Corwin Press, Inc.

25. Collins (1991), p. 153.

26. Riggs, I.M., & Sandlin, R.A. (2000), p. 23.

27. Joint Committee on Standards for Educational Evaluation. (1988). *The personnel evaluation standards*. Newbury Park, CA: Corwin Press.

28. Dallas Public Schools. (1995). *Procedures for developing a teacher portfolio*. (Draft). Dallas, TX: Dallas Public Schools (Research, Planning, and Evaluation Division).

29. Martin-Kneip, G. O. (1999), p. 6.

30. Wolf, K. (1996). Developing an effective teaching portfolio. *Educational Leadership 53*(3), 34–37.

31. National Board for Professional Teaching Standards. (1996). *Middle childhood/generalist standards for National Board certification*. Washington, DC: Author.

32. Oakley, K. (1998).

3

PUTTING PORTFOLIOS INTO ACTION

Well done is better than well said.
Benjamin Franklin

Chapter 2 develops the conceptual foundation for a system of teacher evaluation and professional growth using portfolios. However, as the old adage goes, the devil is in the details. As with any initiative in an organizational setting, you must grapple with, and overcome, the logistical issues that can turn a conceptually valid idea into an unrealized or counterproductive flop. In this chapter, we intend to help teachers and administrators avoid that fate. Specifically, we answer these two questions:

1. What practical tips will help teachers assemble and sustain portfolios?

2. How can a school or school district begin to implement portfolios?

What Practical Tips Will Help Teachers to Assemble and Sustain Portfolios?

Teaching is a complex, multifaceted craft, and teacher portfolios are intended to capture the richness and breadth of the profession. However, the practical considerations of assembling and sustaining a portfolio can be daunting. Creating and maintaining a portfolio requires certain knowledge and abilities. What's more, portfolios are intended to represent the quality of a teacher's performance, not his or her skills in the art of creating a portfolio. It would be unfair, for example, if a skilled, knowledgeable, and effective teacher were evaluated as being poor simply because he or she was not particularly adept at putting together a portfolio. Some practical tips for teachers can help to ensure the validity and reliability of portfolios as a reflection of teachers' skills, knowledge and professional growth.

Assembling a Teacher Portfolio

No matter what the specific purpose or format of a teacher portfolio, there are several steps that are fundamental to creating a portfolio. In the most general terms, knowing where you are going and how to get there are key variables in achieving the goal of creating a meaningful portfolio. The model of implementation in Figure 3.1 is compiled from several sources, among which there is considerable consensus regarding the portfolio process.[1]

Figure 3.1. General Model for the Portfolio Process

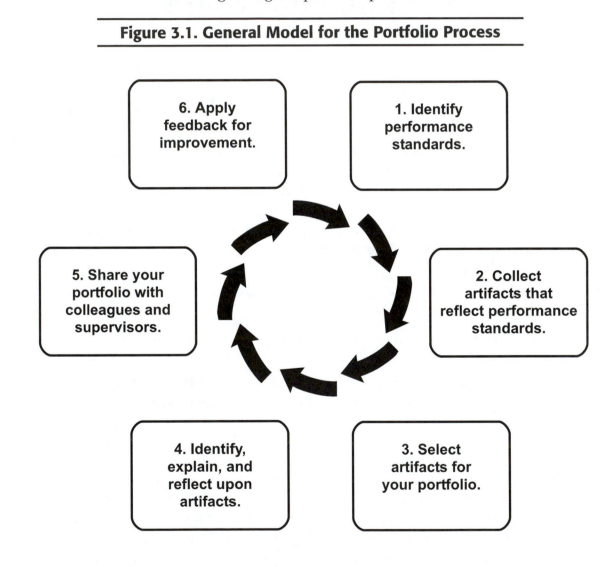

6. Apply feedback for improvement.

1. Identify performance standards.

5. Share your portfolio with colleagues and supervisors.

2. Collect artifacts that reflect performance standards.

4. Identify, explain, and reflect upon artifacts.

3. Select artifacts for your portfolio.

Sustaining a Teacher Portfolio

Figure 3.1 illustrates a linear process that concludes with a feedback loop, which is intended to prompt the process again, continuously. Although this model certainly represents the portfolio process, in reality, the process itself is a good deal messier.

As mentioned earlier, a teacher portfolio is a "living document." One may say that it is a "work in progress." Portfolios should evolve and change over time. The process of creating a teacher portfolio is continuous, theoretically spanning the length of a teacher's career, from pre-service to retirement. Maintaining this whole-career, continuous-improvement, lifelong-learning perspective is no easy task given the daily, sometimes mundane, sometimes extraordinary, challenges of teaching. However, attention to some practical tips for sustaining the portfolio process can make the task more manageable and more meaningful. These tips are captured in Figure 3.2 as headings.

Figure 3.2. Tips For Sustaining a Teacher Portfolio

- ◆ Know what you're going for.
- ◆ Capture the practice.
- ◆ Work on your portfolio over time.
- ◆ Emphasize quality over quantity.
- ◆ Be selective.
- ◆ Collaborate with other professionals.

Know What You're Going For

It may seem obvious, but the centrality of this point requires attention. Teachers need to be well aware of that for which they will be held responsible. In other words, teachers should have a clear, working understanding of the performance standards that their school or district has established. Knowing these in advance and having them firmly fixed in mind enables teachers to continuously identify artifacts that may be included in their portfolios and avoid duplicate or unnecessary effort.

Capture the Practice

Many teachers may view this as the primary task in the development of portfolios, but it is only the beginning of the process when portfolios are used for professional development. Capturing the practice involves designing the layout and organization, collecting relevant artifacts, and writing abstracts or explanations for each artifact. The selection of artifacts should reflect changes in materials or methods used with students that are responsive to previously identified areas of concern. The point is for the portfolio to accurately reflect the reality of the teacher's practice.

Work on Your Portfolio Over Time

Assembling a portfolio in a single sitting is a daunting task! The prospect of sorting through reams of paper, files cabinets, folders, and notebooks, searching for artifacts to document one's performance, can be overwhelming. Assembling a portfolio in a manageable and meaningful way requires a teacher to work on it over time.[2] How much time? The process should ideally follow the academic year, permitting teachers time to collect, select, and organize artifacts simultaneously with the time that these artifacts are being created and used for teaching.[3]

In fact, the process of creating and maintaining one's portfolio should be an integral part of a teacher's regular responsibilities. Professional growth, even evaluation, should not be separate from a teacher's daily work, but should be a part of it. Whether a daily, weekly, monthly, or quarterly collection and assemblage of artifacts is best is probably more a question of personal preference than ideal practice.[4] The point is that a teacher is wise to work on his or her portfolio regularly (i.e., continuously) over time.[5] Some teachers, for example, use expandable folders to collect key documents over time just by dropping them in when the documents are at hand. Periodically, these teachers selectively review their expandable file to decide which of those documents to include in their portfolio and which to discard or file elsewhere.

Emphasize Quality Over Quantity

One of the important steps in assembling a portfolio is to collect a wide array of artifacts and then to select those that best document specific performance standards. Quality is more important than quantity. Less is more. Bigger is not always better. However you phrase it, the point is that portfolios must be limited in size in order to be manageable and meaningful to teachers and to reviewers.

So how large should a portfolio be? How many artifacts are necessary to document a performance standard sufficiently? Opinions vary. Some portfolio advocates recommend no more than one artifact per responsibility.[6] Others recommend no more than three for each required competency.[7] Still others suggest that it takes "five to ten" artifacts to document a goal.[8] A recent study of the use of portfolios in teacher evaluation found that a typical portfolio in the study's sample contained 24 artifacts, which served to document 18 performance standards. The range of artifacts in this study extended from a low of 11 artifacts to a high of 37 in a single portfolio.[9] Such variance is to be expected. Two principles hold true among all of these sources. First, an artifact or two should be sufficient (assuming good quality) in most cases to document a teacher responsibility. You need not attempt to make a case for quality by achieving a critical mass of paper! The second principle is that there are instances when a single document can illustrate multiple responsibilities. For example, a teacher-made lesson plan could serve as evidence in the multiple domains of instructional skills and assessment skills.

A final point bears mentioning regarding the process of *maintaining* a teacher portfolio. We teachers can be notorious pack rats. However, this natural inclination should be vehemently resisted, lest the teacher portfolio become overrun with artifacts. In short, to sustain the viability and relevance of the portfolio, a teacher must be sure to remove superfluous artifacts from his or her portfolio on a regular basis.[10]

Be Selective

Focusing on quality over quantity in choosing artifacts requires some selective discrimination. As we have suggested, portfolios should be used as part of an evaluation system that relies on multiple sources of data regarding teacher performance. Therefore, when selecting artifacts, a teacher should focus on documenting those responsibilities that are not readily illuminated by such sources as observation, student achievement data, or client surveys. In assembling the portfolio, a teacher should focus on those artifacts that are conducive to being exhibited in portfolio format. The next section on selecting artifacts provides considerable guidance to teachers.

Collaborate with Other Professionals

The portfolio process is a powerful tool for self-reflection, but reflection is still more powerful in collaboration. The structure of most schools does not promote sustained interaction among teachers. Portfolios can and should be an impetus for professional collaboration. At every step of the portfolio process, there are opportunities for teachers to share and exchange ideas. Whether discussing the expectations of performance standards, the value of specific artifacts, or other steps in the process, professional collaboration wraps a teacher's portfolio in another layer of evaluation and, therefore, growth.

Collaboration with others at any point in the portfolio development process will enhance a teacher's understanding of his or her teaching practice and how it can be represented to others. As noted by one researcher, "without external input, the capacity of teachers to grow is limited by their own cognitive structures."[11] Colleagues are able to offer objective points of reference and feedback for their fellow teachers to consider as they examine and make sense of their own efforts. The portfolio provides different perspectives on elements of instruction that may have been overlooked or underestimated. Support from others along with new ideas also helps teachers to make a commitment to changing current practice.[12]

Selecting Artifacts

The term "artifact" is perhaps most often associated with the field of archeology, a field in which an artifact is tangible evidence of a past culture. In archeology, artifacts must be genuine to have value. No self-respecting archeologist would manufacture an artifact and attempt to pass it off as being the product of an ancient civilization. A similar mandate holds true in the inclusion of artifacts in a teacher's portfolio. The selection of artifacts should only include items that are actually used in teaching. Artifacts should not be created for purposes of evaluation or presentation alone.

A second important principle of selecting artifacts for inclusion in a teacher's portfolio is that artifacts should be explicitly linked to the professional standards for which a teacher is held accountable. In Chapter 2, we discussed the central role that performance standards have in the evaluation process. Because a teacher is charged with, and held accountable for, meeting these standards, the artifacts that he or she chooses to include in his or her portfolio should directly support and document those standards.

Indeed, teacher choice of content is a key element in implementing portfolios effectively. For example, a recent study of participants in a portfolio evaluation system found that 80 percent of teachers and administrators in the school district view the selection of artifacts by teachers favorably.[13] As another example, Teach for America's Performance Assessment System has teacher selection of artifacts built into the system because teacher choice keeps "teachers invested in the assessment process."[14] The rationale is intuitive. Teachers make hundreds of decisions each day in the classroom. Therefore, who better to decide which artifacts to include in their portfolios than teachers themselves? In fact, not only does the quality of the artifacts reflect on the quality of the teacher, but the quality of the *choices* of artifacts indicates the same, as well.

One author in this area suggests that teacher selection of artifacts is vital to the portfolio process, and offers the following criteria to help guide teachers in their choices:

- An artifact should be relevant to the responsibilities for which a teacher is held accountable.

- An artifact must be authentic.

- An artifact should be reliable as an indicator of the teacher's performance level. In other words, it should demonstrate a certain level of proficiency that is consistent with the level that one might observe in the classroom or through any other means of evaluation.

- An artifact should not demonstrate a performance standard that is more readily obtained through another means of assessment, such as observation or client surveys.

- An artifact should certainly contribute to the process of shedding light on performance. A portfolio, after all, should be an indication of quality, not quantity.

- An artifact should be reasonable to obtain in terms of time and cost.[15]

In this same vein, another writer posits an aid for teachers selecting artifacts for inclusion in professional portfolios. However, he poses these criteria for selecting meaningful artifacts in the form of five guiding questions:

1. Why is this artifact better than other artifacts that I could have chosen?

2. Does this artifact provide evidence of my growth and success against one or more performance standards?

3. Can I rationalize the importance of this artifact to those viewing it out of context?

4. Is this artifact a result of my professional growth and accomplishments?

5. How does this artifact reflect who I am as a teacher?[16]

The number of products and by-products of teaching is vast, and includes lesson plans, assignment sheets, tests, quizzes, scoring rubrics, room charts, learning centers, progress sheets, grade analyses, and much more. The list could go on and on. That is both good and bad news for teachers. It's good in the sense that there are so many artifacts from which a teacher can select to document his or her performance. It's burdensome for the very same reason. However, taken in combination, the two sets of criteria presented above provide guidance to teachers faced with the intimidating task of sifting through the myriad products and by-products of their work as teachers and then deciding which to include in their portfolios as evidence of meeting the performance standards of their schools or districts.

How Can a School or District Begin to Implement Portfolios?

Implementing any new initiative in an organizational setting is a challenge, and this is no less the case with implementing teacher portfolios at the school or district level. Therefore, an individual or committee preparing to take on such a task would do well to review the substantial literature on educational change! A quick summary of the literature concludes that change is usually slow, rarely easy, and typically requires a good deal of effort; not all change is bad, and changes for the better most often have to be orchestrated. But our purpose here is not to review literature. Rather, we provide some practical pointers on implementing teacher portfolios at the school or district level.

Key Questions to Answer Before Implementing Portfolios

This book is designed to guide your use of teacher portfolios as a productive tool for evaluation and professional development. However, there are certain questions that administrators and teachers at the school or district level must ask of themselves when beginning the process of implementing teacher portfolios. This is important because each educational setting is unique, whether in its goals, resources, personnel, culture, or other variables. Therefore, the answers that one gives will also have unique qualities and will affect how you implement portfolios. Figure 3.3 provides a composite list of basic questions to answer *before* implementing teacher portfolios.[17]

Figure 3.3. Key Questions to Answer Before Implementing Portfolios

- What is the purpose of implementing portfolios?

- What standards or responsibilities are portfolios intended to document?

- How will the portfolios be organized? (What will they "look like"?)

- What should portfolios contain?

- How should portfolios be assembled and maintained?

- How will portfolios be reviewed?

Although this text is intended to help you answer these questions, the final answers must be found within your own educational organization and the community you serve.

Steps to Take in Implementing Portfolios

With the key questions answered for the school or district, the process of implementing teacher portfolios is ready to begin. Although we describe this process as "key steps," thereby suggesting a linear process, the truth is that implementation involves a great deal of overlap of steps and repeated starts and stops, depending upon actual progress. In short, implementation is less linear than it is cyclical. Nonetheless, attention to the ten key steps outlined in Figure 3.4, compiled from several sources and from our own experiences in working with school districts, will help to ensure effective implementation of teacher portfolios.[18]

Figure 3.4. Key Steps in Implementing Portfolios

1. Enlist volunteers.
2. Start small.
3. Minimize risk.
4. Offer incentives and support.
5. Study examples of best practice.
6. Allow time for change.
7. Provide training.
8. Conduct field tests and refine.
9. Communicate and collaborate.
10. Evaluate the use of portfolios after implementation.

Enlist Volunteers

Change requires change agents. When implementing teacher portfolios (as with any new initiative), it is good administrative practice to begin by involving a cadre of professionals who are open and amenable to the change. Volunteers are a good source; however, several well-placed "taps on the shoulder" can garner the involvement of certain key staff members in a school or school district who can bring unique experience, skills, or cache to the process. The initial group involved in implementing portfolios should take ownership of the initiative and the process. You will want them to become the strongest advocates of teacher portfolios.

Start Small

Because of the reflective, self-driven nature of teacher portfolios, they require heavy buy-in from teachers. As any administrator will attest, it's difficult to get buy-in when change is dictated. When implementing portfolios, starting with a limited number of participants and widening the sphere of involvement over time is a wise course. Of course, the adjective "small" is relative. When the Fowler Unified School District in California piloted portfolios, they had 18 teachers participate from four of the district's six schools.[19] When the Performance Assessment System was piloted as a component of Teach for America approximately, 200 novice teachers participated.[20] Again, what constitutes "small" is relative. The point is to initiate the use of portfolios with only a fraction of your teaching faculty, with the aim to cultivate the acceptance and use of portfolios over time.

Minimize Risk

As noted above, change is not always welcome; in fact, change is often perceived as a threat. Consequently, it is important to minimize the risk for participants associated with beginning the implementation of portfolios for a school or school district. For example, this could mean temporarily waiving regular evaluation requirements during initial implementation of a portfolio system. The "high stakes" associated with decisions about performance and retention should be delayed to promote involvement in, acceptance of, and constructive feedback about the use of portfolios. Again, the original implementation of the Performance Assessment System serves as a model. When PAS was initiated, all regular consequences associated with the evaluation system were suspended for all volunteers who participated in the initial program

Offer Incentives and Provide Support

If minimizing risks is seeing the glass half empty, then offering incentives and providing support is seeing the glass half full. Reduced risks may not be enough to prompt teachers to participate willingly in initiating teacher portfolios. Even volunteers appreciate rewards for their efforts. Paying teachers a small stipend can be an incentive to participate. But there can be nonmonetary incentives, too. Often teachers are asked to do more with less; therefore, a refreshing change can be simply to provide the necessary resources to support the portfolio initiative, such as notebooks, office supplies, and preparation materials. One of the most important resources for teachers is time. Making arrangements to free up time for teachers to assemble and collaborate regarding their portfolios could be one of the most significant means of support possible.[21] For administrators who are leading the implementation of portfolios, the point is to ensure that the implementation is feasible and rewarding for participants in the initial implementation.

Study Examples of Best Practice

As mentioned previously, every school and school district is unique. No two sets of circumstances are the same; therefore, the implementation of teacher portfolios is not likely to be the same either. Nevertheless, there is a great deal to be learned from the experiences of others, as well as a school or school district's own experiences. When the Washoe County School District in Nevada began the process of implementing portfolios, administrators made a point of having teachers and principals serve as the initial work group that investigated various evaluation models. Notably, at the same time they sought out best practice in their research, they also surveyed themselves and their colleagues to determine what about their previous system of evaluation did *not* work.[22] Establishing the characteristics you want and those that you don't want is a critical step in a school or district's design and implementation of its teacher portfolio system.

Allow Time for Change

As the old cliché goes, "Rome wasn't built in a day." Most significant changes in organizational practices don't occur in a day either. They take time. How much time is required is determined by several factors, including the preferred implementation style (e.g., bottom-up or top-down), acceptance by stakeholders, external factors (e.g., availability of resources), and a host of other possible variables. A realistic window for implementation is one to two years.[23] When the Williamsburg-James City County Public Schools in Virginia revised its evaluation system, the initial process took two full years. Even after a successful pilot program in the third year, the original work group comprised of teachers and administrators continued to work. In fact, the Teacher Evaluation Committee for the district continues to meet and work regularly to refine and improve the evaluation system even after four years of implementation.

Provide Training

The best-designed system is doomed to failure if the people responsible for implementing it do not understand it. This simple truth illustrates the importance of effective training in establishing teacher portfolios as a component of a professional evaluation system. In the Williamsburg-James City County Schools, district-wide training occurred for all teachers in the first full year of implementation. In subsequent years, prior to the start of each new school year, teachers who are new to the district are trained in the portfolio evaluation system as part of their induction to the district.

As important as it is to train the teachers who will be developing portfolios, it is equally important to train the people who are charged with reviewing them. When the Professional Assessment System (PAS) was implemented, all reviewers had to meet certain criteria of experience and training in order to serve in that capacity. The training itself for the PAS involved a two-day, conference-style session. Participants learned about performance standards and the scoring model. They conducted mock portfolio reviews as a group and independently to build inter-rater reliability. Later in the year, a half-day refresher course was required for all reviewers.[24] The PAS initiative provides a good model for the extent that training should take in order to ensure the effectiveness and fairness of a new evaluation system that incorporates teacher portfolios.

An essential component of training is the readily accessible information that can be provided by a portfolio handbook. A portfolio handbook is essentially a how-to guide for teachers addressing the expectations, format, timelines, and processes of the portfolio-based system. The handbook can address the purpose of the portfolio, the role of the portfolio in the evaluation process, procedures for assembling and maintaining a portfolio, the evaluation timeline or cycle, the performance standards, and accepted or required artifacts, just to name the most fundamental contents. "General Guidelines for Organizing a Teacher Portfolio" in Appendix C provides guidelines for teacher portfolios that can provide significant assistance in ensuring that portfolios are used accurately, fairly, usefully, and in a feasible manner.

Conduct Field Tests and
Refine the Portfolio Process

The importance of conducting field tests or pilot programs cannot be overstated. Field tests are akin to taking a car for a test drive before deciding to buy it. This step helps to ensure that everything is in working order before high stakes kick in. Is the selected portfolio format manageable for our teachers? Do the performance standards that we've identified include all of the relevant responsibilities? Have we provided for an appropriate balance of data sources? Is our evaluation timeline feasible? These are just some of the questions that a field test can bring to light. As administrators or a pilot implementation committee address these questions, they can refine the portfolio system to make it more accurate, fair, useful, and feasible.

Communicate and Collaborate

Essential to the entire process of implementing portfolios in an educational organization are communication and collaboration with the many stakeholders that populate the school or school district. Communication, by definition, is a two-way process; therefore, collaboration—that is, the feedback that is received as a result of the initial communication—is fundamental to the process.

Both communication and collaboration should be ongoing processes and should be included in each of the key steps referred to in Figure 3.4. Because the development and implementation of a teacher portfolio system is typically a multiyear process involving ever-increasing numbers of stakeholders, communicating and collaborating cannot be a onetime or discrete step in the process. Rather, administrators or members of a portfolio development committee must give attention to regular and continuous communication and collaboration with others. A "Public Dissemination Plan" in Appendix H provides an example of practical strategies for communicating with the broad public of a school community.

One particularly effective strategy is the dissemination of fact sheets at key points during the development and implementation stages. An example of a fact sheet is illustrated in Figure 3.5 and is also found in Appendix J. Fact sheets permit a uniform, controlled release of information to stakeholder groups, and they also can serve as a prompt for input. These are, after all, the two primary purposes of communicating and collaborating through the implementation process: (a) to build buy-in for teacher portfolios and (b) to garner feedback to refine the proposed system.

Figure 3.5. Sample Focus Group Questions

Accuracy

- Do portfolios provide evidence of professional responsibilities not typically observed in the classroom? If so, in what ways?

Fairness

- Are portfolios a fair means of evaluating teacher performance of professional responsibilities? If so, how?

Usefulness

- Does the development of a portfolio encourage reflection by teachers? If so, in what ways?

Feasibility

- Is the development of portfolios a manageable task for teachers as part of the evaluation process? Why or why not?

Evaluate the Use of Portfolios After Implementation

A final step in the implementation process is the ongoing evaluation of the teacher portfolio program. Is the portfolio system manageable? Do teachers feel that portfolios contribute to their professional growth? Do portfolios aid administrators in making personnel decisions? Do portfolios help to differentiate levels of teacher performance? Is the use of portfolios fair and equitable for all? Do the performance standards reflect the school's or district's model of teacher competency? Do portfolios have a value-added effect on the evaluation process? The possible issues are seemingly endless, and they require considerable attention in order to ensure the effectiveness and fairness of the evaluation system.

Evaluating programs can be a complex task, as the sample questions above indicate. Administrators or members of a portfolio development committee should give careful thought not only to *what* to evaluate but also to *how* to evaluate it. As suggested already, a good communication plan can garner productive feedback, which is a means of evaluating a program's effectiveness. This process can be more formalized by using written surveys or by conducting telephone surveys of randomly selected members of key stakeholder groups. An evaluation survey is found in the appendices. Surveys can result in statistical data regarding impressions, attitudes, and beliefs about the use of teacher portfolios. Another evaluation strategy is the use of focus groups comprised of key stakeholder members. Figure 3.5 is an example of sample focus group questions, which can provide a richness and depth of understanding to the perceived strengths and weaknesses of the teacher portfolio program that may not come across in survey data.

Although determining what evaluative information to collect and how to collect it are key steps in a study of a teacher portfolio program, the final essential step is putting this knowledge to use to improve the program. Ultimately, the use of portfolios is intended to promote effective evaluation and professional development. More importantly, though, one would want to see a link to the ultimate aim of education: Improved student learning and achievement.

Summary

The use of teacher portfolios in evaluation and professional development has a strong conceptual foundation. However, as with any initiative in an organizational setting, the challenges of implementing a new system can overwhelm the best intentions. In this chapter, we have shared practical tips that can help teachers assemble and sustain their portfolios over time. And we have described key questions to answer and essential steps to take when implementing portfolios in a school or school district. Attention to the potential pitfalls of implementation can result in a more efficient and effective portfolio program. We believe that a school or school district that initiates the use of portfolios proactively can reap gains in improved professionalism and increased learning.

References

1. See Cushman, K. (1999). Educators making portfolios: First results from the National School Reform Faculty. *Phi Delta Kappan, 80*(10), 744–750, p. 748; Lyons, N. (1999). How portfolios can shape emerging practice. *Educational Leadership 56*(8), 63–65; Wolf, K. (1994). Teaching portfolios: Capturing the complexities of teaching. In *Valuing teachers' work: New directions in teacher appraisal*. Victoria, Australia: Australian Council for Educational Research, 112–136; and Wolf, K., Lichtenstein, G., & Stevenson, C. (1997). Portfolios in teacher evaluation. In J. H. Stronge (Ed.), *Evaluating teaching: A guide to current thinking and best practice* (pp. 193–214). Thousand Oaks, CA: Corwin Press, pp. 197–198.

2. See Collins, A. (1991). Portfolios for biology teacher assessment. *Journal of Personnel Evaluation in Education, 5,* 147–167; Danielson, C. (2001). New trends in teacher evaluation. *Educational Leadership 58*(5), 12–15; and Williamsburg-James City County Public Schools. (1996). *Teacher Evaluation Handbook.* Williamsburg, VA: Williamsburg-James City County Public Schools.

3. Wolf, K. (1994).

4. Perkins, P. G., & Gelfer, J. I. (1998). Producing teacher/staff portfolios: A method for effective evaluation. *Catalyst for Change, 28*(1), 17–20, p. 19.

5. Riggs, I.M., & Sandlin, R.A. (2000). Teaching portfolios for support of teachers' professional growth. *NASSP Bulletin, 84*(618), 22–27, p.25.

6. Painter, B. (2001). Using teacher portfolios. *Educational Leadership, 58*(5), 31–34, p. 31.

7. National Board for Professional Teaching Standards. (1996). *Middle childhood/generalist standards for National Board certification.* Washington, DC: Author.

8. Wolf, K. (1999). *Leading the professional portfolio process for change.* Arlington, Heights, IL: Skylight, p. 42.

9. Tucker, P. D., Stronge, J. H., Gareis, C. R., & Beers, C. (2000, November). *The use of portfolios in teacher evaluation.* Presented at the annual conference of the University Council of Educational Administration, Albuquerque, NM.

10. Zubizarreta, J. (1994). Teaching portfolios and the beginning teacher. *Phi Delta Kappan, 76*(3), 323–326.

11. Duke, D. L. (1990). Developing teacher evaluation systems that promote professional growth. *Journal of Personnel Evaluation in Education, 4,* 131–144.

12. Dietz, M. E. (1995). Using portfolios as a framework for professional development. *Journal of Staff Development, 16*, 40–43.

13. Peterson, K. D., Walquist, C., Boone, K., Thompson, J., & Chatterton, K. (2001). Using more data sources to evaluate teachers. *Educational Leadership, 58*(5), 40–43.

14. Oakley, K. (1998). The Performance Assessment System: A portfolio assessment model for evaluating beginning teachers. *Journal of Personnel Evaluation in Education, 11*, 323–341, p. 327.

15. Wheeler, P. H. (1994). *The advantages and disadvantages of using portfolios in teacher evaluation* (Tempo C Memo 14). Kalamazoo, MI: Western Michigan University, The Evaluation Center, Center for Research on Educational Accountability and Teacher Evaluation, p. 18.

16. Painter, B. (2001).

17. See Perkins, P. G., & Gelfer, J. I. (1998), p. 17; Stowell, L. P., McDaniel, J. E., Rios, F. A., & Kelly, M. G. (1993). Casting wide the net: Portfolio assessment in teacher education. *Middle School Journal, 25*(2), 61–66; and Wolf, K. (1991). The schoolteacher's portfolio: Issues in design, implementation, and evaluation. *Phi Delta Kappan, 73*, 129–136.

18. See Doolittle, P. (1994). Teacher portfolio assessment. *ERIC/AE Digest* (EDO–TM–94–07). Washington, DC: ERIC Clearinghouse on Assessment and Evaluation; Martin-Kneip, G. O. (1999). *Capturing the wisdom of practice.* Alexandria, VA: Association for Supervision and Curriculum Development; Sawyer, L. (2001). Revamping a teacher evaluation system. *Educational Leadership, 58*(5), 44–47; Wolf, K. (1999), p. 84; Wolf, K., Lichtenstein, G., & Stevenson, C. (1997), pp. 209 & 212.

19. Curry, S., & Cruz, J. (2000). Portfolio-based teacher assessment. *Thrust for Educational Leadership, 29*(3), 34–37.

20. Oakley, K. (1998).

21. Curry, S., & Cruz, J. (2000).

22. Sawyer, L. (2001), pp. 45–46.

23. See Doolittle, P. (1994); and Martin–Kneip, G. O. (1999).

24. Oakley, K. (1998).

4

TEACHER PORTFOLIOS AND TEACHER EVALUATION

We are what we repeatedly do.
Excellence, then, is not an act, but a habit.

Aristotle

"If 'a picture paints a thousand words,' then what's a videotape worth?" A few years ago, a teacher pondered this rhetorical question as a committee of teachers was discussing the school district's teacher evaluation system. Consisting largely of a prescriptive checklist of lesson components associated with a model of direct instruction, the school district's previous evaluation system was receiving broad criticism. Teachers complained that the evaluation tool did not allow for their increasing reliance upon cooperative learning strategies and other student-centered models of instruction. It seemed to ignore the fact that not all lessons are isolated packages of instruction that conclude with a neatly tied ribbon called "closure." Moreover, the existing evaluation checklist was almost entirely a prescriptive process for teaching that ignored the results (i.e., student learning) of teaching. And, as illustrated by the teacher's comment above, a "snapshot" observation of a classroom simply could not capture the myriad responsibilities required of a teacher both inside and outside of the classroom. The teacher's point: "I need to videotape my entire *day* for my principal to see all that I do!"

What's more, in the above instance, principals and administrators shared the teacher's concerns. They, too, criticized the narrow instructional model on which the evaluation was based, a problem that could be addressed by redefining teachers' instructional responsibilities more broadly and less prescriptively. Yet, principals and administrators also wanted a vehicle for accounting for, and recognizing, not only the instructional responsibilities of teaching, but also the many related responsibilities such as planning, assessment, management, and

55

professionalism that support excellence in teaching. This was the content of the teacher's hypothetical videotape. After all, if your teacher evaluation system is based primarily on a limited formal observation of instruction in the classroom, how does an evaluator "observe" everything else that goes into being a teacher? Can all of the important duties and responsibilities of teachers be observed, or are there other means to better capture the essence of quality teaching? In an attempt to answer these questions, in this chapter we explore the following issues related to the use of teacher portfolios in teacher evaluation:

♦ What are alternatives to observation-only teacher evaluation systems?

♦ Do teacher portfolios contribute to a valid assessment of teacher performance?

♦ Do portfolios have a value-added effect on teacher evaluation?

♦ What are additional benefits in using portfolios in teacher evaluation?

♦ What are guidelines for using portfolios in teacher evaluation?

What Are Alternatives to Observation-Only Teacher Evaluation Systems?

A teacher evaluation system that relies primarily on formal observation is unbalanced: it just isn't possible to get a full, fair, or even accurate picture of a teacher's performance merely with classroom visits—even with visits more frequent than two or three times a year. We offer the following key points to support this contention:

♦ *Direct observation* as the sole basis for performance evaluation has limited utility and can even be questioned as a valid and reliable means of evaluating classroom teachers and other educators.

♦ The *complexity of professional roles* in today's schools requires a performance evaluation that reflects that complexity.

♦ *Multi-faceted data collection*, the use of evaluative input from multiple sources, including portfolios, enables the evaluator to obtain a much more richly textured performance portrait of the teacher.

♦ An *expanded performance portrait* is highly desirable, if not necessary, for high-quality teacher evaluation. By collecting and analyzing responses from the numerous constituencies with whom an educator works and by analyzing the artifacts collected in a portfolio, the evaluator can develop an evaluation based on an expanded knowledge of the teacher's work, thus enhancing the validity and reliability of that evaluation.

Much of the data collected to provide insight into a teacher's performance can and should be collected by the teacher. When additional teacher performance data are collected and analyzed as a systematic part of the evaluation process, especially contributions invited from others, such as parents and students, it is important to provide a means for collecting and using these data. For example, Figure 4.1 shows a sample student survey that can be included as part of a multiple data source evaluation system, the results of which can be included in a portfolio.

Figure 4.1. Sample Items from Student Survey (Grades 4–5)

		Yes	Sometimes	No
1.	My teacher listens to me.			
2.	My teacher gives me help when I need it.			
3.	My teacher shows us how to do new things.			
4.	I know what I am supposed to do in class.			
5.	I am able to do the work in class.			

The addition of client surveys is a significant step in extending the sources of information regarding teacher performance. When coupled with portfolio development and observation, the teacher, the supervisor, and the client all have a voice in the evaluative process.

It is important to recognize that materials and information that a teacher contributes to the performance portfolios doesn't necessarily entail significant additional record keeping. Rather, the use of materials generated, and records maintained, in the natural course of fulfilling specific teaching job responsibilities should be emphasized. If a portfolio becomes merely a paper chase, it invariably misses the marks of professional growth and improved performance evaluations.

Do Teacher Portfolios Contribute to a Valid Assessment of Teacher Performance?

The validity of teacher performance evaluation is increased almost by definition when we increase the number and types of performance being evaluated. The information used in making decisions about personnel should be a valid measure of *actual* job performance and, thus, should include information on all major dimensions of the job. Multifaceted data sources in the evaluation of teachers enhance validity of the total evaluation process by using a variety of indicators of performance toward the accomplishment of teaching goals and provide more accurate information than collecting a single example of performance possibly could.[1] If we collect information on all major dimensions of a teacher's job using portfolios and other forms of data, in conjunction with classroom observations, then we enhance the validity of the information reviewed in the process, the sampling of those items, and the very legitimacy, or construct validity, of the evaluation system itself.[2]

Validity of Portfolios: A Case Study

The findings of our research suggest that portfolios can document the fulfillment of teaching responsibilities considerably better than observation-only evaluation systems. In one study of the value of portfolios for teacher evaluation[3], independent raters reviewed 24 portfolios of a random stratified sample of selected teachers taken from a school district that mandates the use of teacher portfolios in its evaluation system. The raters judged the relevancy of the portfolio contents based on teachers' defined job responsibilities. Inter-rater reliability was established for data coding and a matrix of the 18 job responsibilities and 37 artifact types was created to record documents.

The reviewers found fully 90 percent of all artifacts had content validity and only 10 percent were superfluous. The content analysis of the portfolios found that the four broad domains in the teacher evaluation system were each documented in the teachers' portfolios. Specifically, teachers in the sample included an average of 24 valid artifacts in their portfolios that demonstrated performance in the domains of instruction, assessment, management, and professionalism. Figure 4.2 depicts the average number of artifacts used to document each domain.

Not surprisingly, certain teacher domains were more readily documented in the portfolios than others. Teachers most frequently documented the domain of professionalism, whereas the domains of instruction, assessment, and classroom management were less frequently documented. Further statistical analysis in the study found that the areas of instruction and classroom management in particular proved to be least conducive to documentation in the portfolio—although, notably nearly half of the teachers in the sample were able to document their performance in these areas.

At first blush, the variance among the four domains may seem problematic, but the fact actually illustrates one of the purposes of including portfolios in a multiple data source system of evaluation: namely, portfolios enhance the documentation of those teaching responsibilities not readily observable by others during formal observations in the classroom and informal interactions in other settings. In fact, the results of this study reveal the following key findings:

Figure 4.2. Mean Number of Artifacts

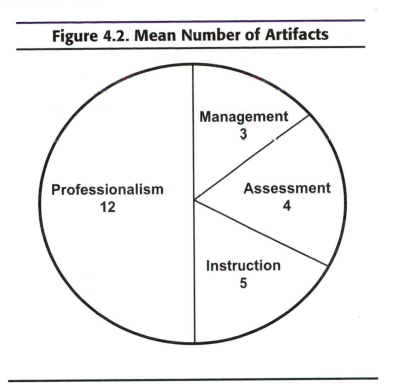

- Classroom observations and performance portfolios go hand-in-hand for documenting teacher job performance.

- Classroom observations appear to better document the teaching domain of classroom management, whereas portfolios tend to better document the domains of assessment and professionalism.

- Both classroom observations and portfolios provide valuable documentation for instruction.

- Lesson plans and units were some of the most frequently used types of artifacts to document fulfillment of instructional responsibilities.

- Complete units of study that included plans, instructional strategies, rubrics for assessment, and samples of student work were found to be the richest source of insight on the teacher's practice, as they reflected the integrative craft of teaching.

- Portfolio artifacts with reflective annotations or explanations of how the artifacts related to teaching were most helpful in explaining intent and learning by the teacher.

- Student work and evidence of student learning was useful in portraying the results of the teacher's work.

Overall, teachers selected meaningful documents to demonstrate their work in the domains of instruction, assessment, classroom management, and professionalism. A total of 46 separate types of artifacts were identified as valid by the panel of raters. There were "preferred" artifacts in each domain that more teachers tended to use than others. In instruction, the most frequently included artifact was a lesson plan or unit. In assessment, the majority of the teachers used examples of assessment measures. In the area of classroom management, teachers tended to include their classroom management philosophy. And in the domain of professionalism, teachers favored examples of their correspondence with parents as evidence.

We were concerned about the possible disparity between tenured and untenured teachers in their ability to collect and present material in their portfolios. Interestingly, there was little variance between the number of artifacts in the portfolios of tenured and nontenured teachers. Tenured teachers included an average of 25 artifacts in their portfolios, whereas nontenured teachers had an average of 22 artifacts—not a significant difference. However, tenured teachers were seven times more likely to include lesson plans and comprehensive units of study than nontenured teachers, and tenured teachers included assessment measures four times more often. These findings indicate some differentiation between tenured and nontenured teachers related to the availability of certain artifacts. Nevertheless, the portfolios of both experienced and new teachers enabled the documentation of the less-readily observable teacher responsibilities in assessment and professionalism, providing an important evaluative complement to the traditional observation of instruction and management.

Validity of Portfolios: Additional Evidence

Enhanced Validity and the Use of Multiple Data Sources

Traditional teacher evaluation rubrics that rely on limited data drawn from a single source are limited in their validity (that is, their ability to accurately assess and portray teaching performance). As one researcher noted in advocating the use of portfolios in teacher evaluation, "Current practices serve neither the novice nor the experienced teacher to any meaningful extent."[4] In particular, traditional teacher evaluation practices have limited value in either holding teachers accountable or in helping them develop professionally.

To remedy this problem, "a teacher evaluation system should have more than one way to collect data and should rely on more than one source of data (e.g., observations by peers, ratings by students and parents, interviews by principals)."[5] In Figure 4.3, we provide a matrix of how multiple data sources that often are included in performance portfolios can be integrated into an evaluation system that more comprehensively and, consequently, more validly,

Figure 4.3. Teacher Evaluation Data Sources Matrix

Teacher Job Responsibility	Observations	Portfolio Review	Client Surveys	Student Achievement	Examples of Additional Data
Preparation for Instruction	P	S		P	◆ Lesson plan
Instructional Delivery	P			P	◆ Peer observation
Management of Learning Environment	P		S	S	◆ Discipline referrals ◆ Parent/student feedback
Assessment of Student Achievement	S	P		P	◆ Test data ◆ Grade book ◆ Report cards
Communications: Students	P	S	P		◆ Informal feedback
Communications and Community Relations	P	S	P		◆ Parent feedback
Professional Responsibilities	P	P			◆ Formal and informal correspondence ◆ Extra-curricular activities

Key: P—Primary source; S—Secondary source; Blank—Minor, or not a source documents teacher performance. (More detailed matrices of how data sources can be matched to teacher performance responsibilities are included in the appendices.)

Balancing Process and Product in Teacher Evaluation

Another impediment to valid teacher evaluations is the overdependence on assessing process variables such as questioning skills and differentiation. It isn't that teaching processes shouldn't be evaluated; rather, it's that the *processes* should be connected to *results*. In fact, evaluations that are constructed as stylistic or teacher attribute checklists and that look almost singularly at selected *processes* of teaching while ignoring the *results* of teaching have limited value or validity in assessing teacher effectiveness. As a solution to this problem of process imbalance in teacher evaluation, portfolios can "...link teaching to student learning by including student outcomes in addition to teaching documentation."[6]

Describing the use of portfolio assessment in the Performance Assessment System, a teacher evaluation approach originally developed by Teach for America, it was explained that "teachers demonstrate their teaching performance through a portfolio with multiple strands of evidence that collectively depict the teacher's approach and effectiveness at increasing student learning."[7] Figure 4.4 depicts a teacher evaluation design that balances and integrates the processes, or instructional aspects of teaching, with the products, or student outcomes of teaching, and, thus, improves the validity of the assessment and the value of the results obtained from the assessment.

Figure 4.4. Evaluation Design that Integrates Processes with Products

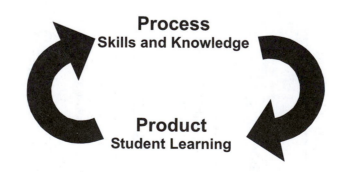

Process
Skills and Knowledge

Product
Student Learning

Do Portfolios Have a Value-Added Effect on Teacher Evaluation?

Are teacher portfolios just another bandwagon for educators, or do they add real value to performance evaluation? In particular, do portfolio-based teacher evaluations do a better job than traditional single-source evaluations in differentiating outstanding teaching from acceptable teaching, and acceptable teaching from unacceptable teaching?

Differentiating Performance in Teacher Evaluation

Do portfolios help evaluators distinguish between more effective and less effective teachers? After all, if teachers are to improve their capacity to be effective in the classroom, it will be through the identification of relative strengths and weaknesses, and then encouraging those areas of strength and improving those areas in need. To answer the question, we found evidence from both the National Board for Professional Teaching Standards and from a study of portfolio use in a single school district that, yes, portfolios do seem to make a difference.

Differentiating Teacher Effectiveness: The National Board Study

The National Board for Professional Teaching Standards (NBPTS) has relied heavily on a portfolio evaluation system since its inception in 1987. The NBPTS has established standards for the advanced certification of teachers in 20 different fields and has certified over 10,000 teachers thus far.[8] It is an "extraordinarily complex and ambitious performance assessment of teaching" composed of "six site-based portfolios exercises and four on-demand assessment center exercises."[9] In addition to the submission of two videotapes of their teaching with the whole class and in small groups, candidates must submit and analyze samples of student work as a reflection of their instructional expertise. It is reported to be an all-consuming task that requires approximately one year to complete, but most teachers report that it offers an incomparable professionalizing experience.[10]

In a recent comprehensive study of the certification system, researchers at the University of North Carolina at Greensboro examined the validity of the NBPTS assessment process. Specifically, they asked the question, "Can National Board Certified teachers and their noncertified counterparts be distinguished on the basis of the quality of work produced by their students?"[11] The researchers reviewed instructional lesson plans, made observational visits to the classrooms, and analyzed samples of student work for 65 teachers. They found that the National Board Certified teachers in this sample obtained higher mean scores on all 13 "attributes of expert teaching that have emerged from the ever-expanding body of research on teaching and learning"[12] than did the noncertified teachers and with statistically significant differences on 11 of the 13 comparisons. The students of Board Certified teachers also exhibited differences from those of noncertified teachers. In their submitted work, they showed "an understanding of the concepts targeted in instruction that [was] more integrated, more coherent, and a higher level of abstraction than understandings achieved by other students."[13]

Differentiating Summative Results: A School District Study

One criticism of many teacher evaluation systems has been the reality that the large majority of teachers are rated at the highest rating available. When all teachers are judged to be equally outstanding, it tends to undermine the evaluation system's credibility and bankrupts the value of an authentically high rating.

There are many truly outstanding teachers in our schools and they should be recognized. However, deeming 96 percent of the instructional staff as above average seems dubious in any school system, but this was the finding from the case study cited earlier in this chapter.[14] Based on a historical review of all evaluation ratings, we found that in one year 75 percent of the teachers were rated as "outstanding," and an additional 21 percent were judged to be "commendable," with only 4 percent labeled "acceptable" and 0 percent "needing improvement." No one was found "unacceptable." Comparable results were found for the following school year.

With the introduction of performance portfolios in this school district, associated training, and the heightened attention given to teacher evaluation, there was significantly greater differentiation in evaluation ratings among teachers as shown in Figure 4.5. Under the new teacher evaluation system, a similar review of all evaluations for teachers found that 43 percent of teachers were judged to be "exceeding expectations," 55 percent were judged to be "meeting expectations," 1.6 percent "needed improvement," and 0.1 percent were adjudged "unsatisfactory." Although the new system with portfolios did not reveal large numbers of underperforming teachers, it did help administrators better discriminate between capable teachers and truly exceptional ones. Our supposition is that with more information available to them in the evaluation process, namely the portfolio, principals were able to recognize those teachers who went above and beyond the job requirements and those who did the job capably. We cannot fully credit portfolios with this change in outcomes, but they do contribute to an evaluation system that promotes and recognizes professional excellence.

Figure 4.5. Summative Results

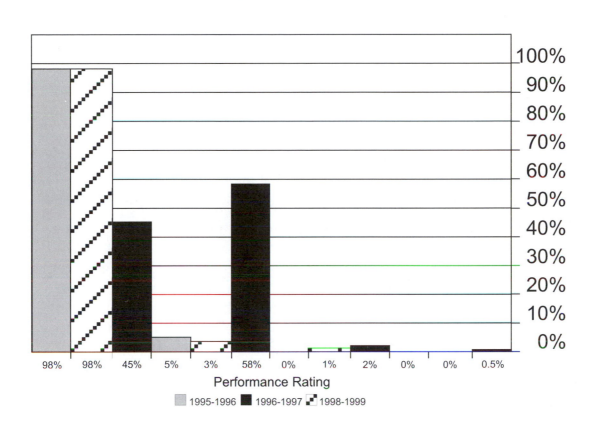

Performance Rating

1995-1996 ■ 1996-1997 ▨ 1998-1999

What Are Additional Benefits in Using Portfolios in Teacher Evaluation?

Given the multifaceted nature of teaching today, it seems almost transparently obvious that their performance should be documented with multiple data sources. Additionally, there are numerous advantages to collecting performance evaluation data from a variety of sources. Some of these advantages include:

♦ *Increased reliability*: Reliability typically increases with an increase in sampling size. Therefore, evaluations based on multiple data sources, including portfolios, can improve the reliability of the evaluation as compared with one-shot formal observations because of the increased sampling of performance from multiple perspectives. Additionally, with more broadly based evaluative input, there is an increased likelihood that performance strengths and weaknesses can be identified and corroborated by several sources of data.

◆ *Decreased subjectivity*: The evaluator bases the teacher's evaluation not solely on one or more direct observations but on the entire performance portrait, including information assimilated and provided by the teacher via the portfolio. Additionally, information from the teacher's students, peers, and others with whom the teacher works can be included in the portfolio.

◆ *Increased comfort level*: By removing the sole burden placed on the evaluator to collect all performance data, both the evaluator and the teacher can have more confidence that evaluations are a fair representation of the various strengths and contributions of the teacher.

◆ *Improved self-evaluation*: Connecting teacher portfolios to evaluation isn't just for the purposes of external summative evaluation: the connection also serves well to improve the teacher's opportunity to self-evaluate. "If the portfolio is structured around sound professional standards that include the accountability goals of the school system and the individual school, the portfolio is an excellent way to help teachers gauge their effectiveness."[15]

◆ *Increased professionalism*: Under traditional teacher evaluation models, the evaluator essentially serves as an "inspector" of performance, a role that is deprofessionalizing and passive for the teacher. "As long as teacher evaluation is something done *to* teachers by administrators, it will continue to reinforce a model of teaching that discourages teachers' initiative in exercising their own critical professional judgment."[16] Conversely, when teachers have an active voice in presenting evidence regarding what they do and how well they do it, they assume a role in evaluation similar to other professions, such as architects—a role that encourages personal ownership for improvement and professional growth.

◆ *Expanded performance portrait*: With input from job artifacts, self-assessment, and feedback from those with whom the teacher works, a performance picture unfolds that is both broader and deeper than one based on one individual's observation of a brief performance "event." Additionally, by incorporating assessment of both in-class and out-of-class activities, portfolios help provide important input that is often omitted from classroom-based observations.

What Are Guidelines for Developing and Using Portfolios in Teacher Evaluation?

In Chapter 3, we shared some practical steps for implementing teacher portfolios in a school or district setting. Drawn from the literature on teacher evaluation and portfolios assessment, here we offer additional tips that can be useful in planning and implementing a performance evaluation system that incorporates teacher portfolios as an important component in a quality teacher evaluation system. Although these guidelines echo the steps outlined in Chapter 3, they specifically address the inclusion of portfolios for distinguishing the variations in *quality* of teacher performance.

- *Communication is critically important in teacher evaluation.* Grant Wiggins[17] in writing about the use of portfolio assessment with students, made a point that is germane to our discussion of the use of portfolios with teachers: procedures must be developed through a collaborative, public forum in which the audience and client are involved. Throughout the teacher evaluation process, including the development of procedures for use of portfolios, teachers have every right to be involved in, and to know about, the evaluation system as much as possible. Additionally, the portfolio can serve as a vehicle for enhancing conversations regarding performance throughout the evaluation process.

- *Relate the overall teacher evaluation system and individual performance roles to goals of the organization.* Designing a teacher evaluation system that relies on authentic data, such as portfolios, must begin by matching the goals of the school or school system with the needs of students, teachers, administrators, parents, and the larger community. In fact, determining the needs of the organization is a prerequisite for all remaining steps if the evaluation process is to be relevant to the organization's mission and, ultimately, responsive to the public demands for accountability.

- *The context of teacher evaluation must be taken into account.* Understanding and accounting for the context of teacher evaluation is another critical factor in developing sound evaluation systems.[18] A few suggestions in this regard include:

  - Data collection should be context-specific and based on real job performance.

- Authentic assessment, such as in performance portfolios, should be composed of real instances of *criterion-based*, extended performances.[19]

- Authentic assessment with teacher portfolios involves frequent, brief evaluations of work that evolve from, and are tied to, curricular objectives and content.[20]

- The teacher's evaluation should not be a one-shot formal classroom observation, but rather an ongoing, systematic data collection, formal and informal, over time.

♦ *Base the teacher evaluation on clearly defined job duties.* In general, performance evaluation needs to be built upon clear and reasonable duties of the teacher.[21] In other words, evaluate the teacher on what she or he was hired to do.

The detailed "Performance Standards" in Appendix A can be used to clarify the job expectations of the teacher. Additionally, the teacher performance standards become the framework for organizing the portfolio and presenting evidence of performance.

♦ *A performance assessment rubric must be used to make fair judgments in teacher evaluation.* Setting standards involves determining appropriate levels of performance, such as meeting expectations, exceeding expectations, or needing improvement. Procedures for the use of performance portfolios must include clearly stated performance expectations to which everyone in the school aspires. It is important that the process for interpreting data collected from a variety of sources be well understood and consistently implemented in order to ensure fairness and legal defensibility.

A Performance Assessment Rubric (PAR) is included in Appendix B and is designed to serve as a detailed scoring rubric for the set of teacher performance responsibilities also included in the appendices and described above. Used in conjunction with one another, the set of teacher responsibilities and the PAR answer two vital questions in the teacher evaluation process:

- What are the job expectations or the teacher performance standards?

- What is the expected level of performance for each major job responsibility?

Figure 4.6 offers an example of how a teacher performance responsibility is related to the Performance Assessment Rubric. The application of the PAR to the given teacher performance responsibility provides a useful means for assessing the teacher portfolio and other applicable evidence in light of expected performance standards.

Figure 4.6. Sample Teacher Performance Responsibility and Performance Appraisal Rubric

Domain: Instruction

I-6: The teacher uses a variety of instructional strategies to promote student learning.

Performance Rubric

Exemplary	Satisfactory	Needs Improvement	Unsatisfactory
The teacher develops and uses a variety of instructional strategies to promote student learning.	The teacher uses a variety of instructional strategies to promote student learning.	The teacher uses a limited variety of instructional strategies that do not target the needs of most students.	The teacher's instructional strategies are ineffective and/or inappropriate on a regular basis.

◆ *The overall teacher evaluation system should facilitate professional growth.* Evaluation with an improvement orientation is intended to provide recognition for noteworthy performance, along with immediate and intermediate feedback for performance improvement and assistance when needed. A total evaluation system can ultimately lead to improved performance by the teacher as well as enhanced performance of the teacher's students. The use of portfolios contributes significantly to this overall effort in that it broadens the evaluator's and teacher's awareness of what has been accomplished and where specific strengths and weaknesses in performance exist. This recognition, in turn, can lead to improvement strategies, improved teacher performance, and, ultimately, improved student performance. We describe the importance of using portfolios for professional growth in Chapter 5.

Summary

In the final analysis, teacher evaluation is a process for determining how an individual, program, or school is performing in relation to a given set of circumstances, such as the mission of the organization, individual objectives, and the available resources. When the judgments that are made in this process are viewed as endpoints, versus the beginning points of an ongoing dialogue between a supervisor and teacher, evaluation becomes irrelevant. Evaluation that is conducted in a superficial manner with little or no resource allocation, using invalid evaluation systems and flawed implementation designs, deprives the school, its employees, and the public-at-large of opportunities for improvement and the benefits that professional growth and accountability afford. "All of us, whatever our relationship to the educational enterprise, deserve high-quality evaluation. An evaluation system that is built squarely upon individual *and* institutional improvement holds the promise of filling this need."[22] Teacher portfolios can contribute to a better evaluation.

In this chapter on the use of performance portfolios as a key component in teacher evaluation, we are not suggesting the elimination of classroom observations; indeed, observations serve a valuable role in assessing performance. Rather, we are encouraging the use of multiple data sources, with a particular focus on performance portfolios, in order to develop a fuller, more accurate picture of performance. The portfolio is a vehicle for gaining insight into a teacher's performance. It can be eye-opening for the teacher; after all, there is no more powerful evaluation than that which we provide for ourselves through self-reflection. Additionally, portfolios can be insightful for the supervisor; by better understanding the processes and products of teaching, the supervisor can develop a better appreciation for the teacher's work and provide better guidance and more valuable assistance to the teacher.

Another key principle to remember in the use of portfolios in teacher evaluation is that collecting feedback regarding teacher performance from a variety of sources is not synonymous with evaluation; it is merely the collection of information upon which the evaluation will be based. There is no value in grading a document. It is not the portfolio that is being assessed; it is the teacher as a professional.

Finally, and most importantly, understandings gleaned from developing and reviewing the teacher's performance portfolio can (and should) support individualized professional development. After all, the real value in evaluation is continuous, sustained improvement that leads to improved teaching, and, ultimately, to improved learning. We expand on the significant role of professional development in the next chapter.

References

1. Valencia, S. (1990). A portfolio approach to classroom reading assessment: The whys, whats and hows. *Reading Teacher, 43*, 338–340.

2. Shulman, L. S. (1988). A union of insufficiencies: Strategies for teacher assessment in a periof of reform. *Educational Leadership, 46*(3), 36–41.

3. Beers, C., Stronge, J. H., Tucker, P. D., & Gareis, C. (2000, March). *How effective are portfolios in teacher evaluation?* Paper presented at the annual convention of the Association of Supervision and Curriculum Development, New Orleans, LA.

4. Regan, H. B. (1993). Integrated portfolios as tools for differentiated teacher evaluation: A proposal. *Journal of Personnel Evaluation in Education, 7*, 275–290, p. 275.

5. Wheeler, P.H. (1993). *Using portfolios to assess teacher performance* (EREAPA Publication Series 93–97). Livermore, CA: EREAPA Associates. (ERIC Document Reproduction Service No. ED 361 967)

6. Regan, H. B. (1993). p. 277.

7. Oakley, K. (1998). The performance assessment system: A portfolio assessment model for evaluating beginning teachers. *Journal of Personnel Evaluation in Education, 11*, 323–341, p. 323.

8. Harman, A. E. (2001). A wider role for the National Board. *Educational Leadership, 58*(8), 54–55.

9. Bond, L., Smith, T., Baker, W. K., & Hattie, J. A. (2000). *The certification system of the National Board for Professional Teaching Standards: A construct and consequential validity study.* Greensboro, NC: Center for Educational Research and Evaluation, The University of North Carolina at Greensboro.

10. Bohen, D. B. (2001). Strengthening teachers through national certification. *Educational Leadership, 58*(8), 50–53.

11. Bond, L., Smith, T., Baker, W. K., & Hattie, J. A. (2000), p. viii.

12. Bond, L., Smith, T., Baker, W. K., & Hattie, J. A. (2000), p. ix.

13. Bond, L., Smith, T., Baker, W. K., & Hattie, J. A. (2000), p. x.

14. Beers, C., Stronge, J. H., Tucker, P. D., & Gareis, C. (1999).

15. Curry, S., & Cruz, J. (2000, January/February). Portfolio-based teacher assessment. *Thrust for Educational Leadership, 29*(3), 34–37, p. 34.

16. Stone, B., & Mata, S. (1996, April). *Capturing the whole picture: Portfolios and professional conversations in teacher evaluation.* Paper presented at the annual meeting of the American Educational Research Association, New York, p. 1.

17. Wiggins, G. (1991). Standards, not standardization: Evolving quality student work. *Educational Leadership, 48*(4), 18–26.

18. Stufflebeam, D. L. (1983). The CIPP model for program evaluation. In G. Madaus, M. S. Scriven, & D. L. Stufflebeam (Eds.), *Evaluation models: Viewpoints on educational and human services in evaluation* (pp. 117–141). Boston: Kluwer-Nijhoff.

19. Kirst, M. W. (1991). Interview on assessment issues with James Popham. *Educational Researcher, 20*(2), 24–27.

20. Green, K. E. (1991). *Educational Testing: Issues and Applications.* New York: Garland.

21. Scriven, M. (1994). Duties of the teacher. *Journal of Personnel Evaluation in Education, 8,* 151–184.

22. Stronge, J. H. (1995). Balancing individual and institutional goals in educational personnel evaluation: A conceptual framework. *Studies in Educational Evaluation, 21,* 131–152.

5

TEACHER PORTFOLIOS AND PROFESSIONAL DEVELOPMENT

The unexamined life is not worth living.
Socrates

The teaching portfolio is one supervisory tool that is truly capable of serving the dual purposes of evaluation and professional development. Although we view the two purposes as mutually supportive and beneficial, we acknowledge that there is a greater sense of freedom and risk taking associated with using portfolios strictly for professional development. When portfolios are used for evaluation, there is an expectation for the educator to provide evidence and document competence. Consequently, the portfolio often becomes a collection of the teacher's finest work and his or her students' best products. Although all of us would like to be judged by our most impressive work, a narrow focus on strengths seldom assists us in improving our skills and knowledge.

When portfolios are used exclusively for professional development, they permit more latitude to examine a range of teaching efforts, from the unsuccessful to the most exciting, and the resulting impact on student learning. This freedom from perceived judgment can encourage greater risk taking and reflection on the *what*, *why*, and *how* of successful teaching. When a teacher feels safe, the use of the portfolio can encourage greater awareness of one's work with students, more opportunities for analysis and self-critique, and a clearer understanding of how to judge one's own instructional improvement. In this chapter, we explore the following questions related to the use of portfolios for professional growth:

♦ Why use portfolios for professional development?

♦ What is the relationship between reflection and professional development?

♦ How does reflection contribute to professional development?

73

◆ What is the format of a portfolio for professional development?

◆ How do educators perceive the use of portfolios for professional development?

Why Use Portfolios for Professional Development?

Many of the large-scale portfolio efforts in the country, such as the National Board for Professional Teaching Standards and Connecticut's Beginning Educator Support and Training Program, successfully combine evaluation and professional development as the goals of their systems. The National School Reform Faculty, however, has introduced the use of portfolios to teachers and administrators in their schools with the sole intention of fostering professional development that will create ripple effects of fundamental improvement.

Case in Point: The National School Reform Faculty

One of the more visible and successful examples of using portfolios for professional development has been the work of the National School Reform Faculty (NSRF) under the aegis of the Annenberg Institute for School Reform. The NSRF advocates the use of portfolios as a means for "critical friends" groups to discuss their professional work in a deep and meaningful way. The critical friends groups are composed of teachers and administrators who meet regularly with a "coach" to talk about their current practice and how to improve student learning as part of their school-wide reform efforts.[1]

Beginning in 1995, the NSRF encouraged each critical friends group to develop standards for adult and student learning and then to use portfolios "to present, examine, and reflect on their own work in the context of those standards."[2] Reflection and learning were intended to be a collaborative effort among educators at common sites and across a network of schools. Although the NSRF did not recommend a structure for the portfolios, other than that portfolios address locally developed standards, common elements of the first portfolios included examples of teacher and student work, a central purpose or question, and evidence of professional growth.

The portfolios developed by members of the critical friends groups were then presented to each other and, in some cases, other educators at NSRF conferences. To create a sense of emotional safety for the presenters, a carefully crafted structure was established for the review and discussion of each portfolio. The protocols encouraged a careful examination of specific portfolio elements and a constructive feedback process. The ultimate goal for the NSRF is to create and nurture the professional dialogue within and across schools that portfolios permit by capturing the practice of teachers and administrators. Professional inquiry about teaching practice is viewed as a way to improve both teacher and student learning. Summing up his experience, one teacher said "[the portfolio] forces me to constantly and consistently look at what I'm doing, making sure that what I'm doing is good—for students and for me—and to improve."[3]

Not only are portfolios beneficial to the professional development of experienced teachers, they also have been found to be a highly effective tool in developing more reflective and responsive beginning teachers. Teacher preparation programs in a wide range of areas, including reading, TESOL (Teaching English to Speakers of Other Languages), and biology,[4] have begun using portfolios to establish the habit of inquiry that promotes self-examination and reflection about teaching practice. According to survey research regarding teacher education programs, "pre-service teachers who use portfolios are more knowledgeable about issues related to the complexities of teaching, about using portfolios as an assessment tool, and about understanding that learning is an ongoing process."[5] Portfolios empower teachers at all developmental stages to take charge of their own learning by capturing the teaching act and its impact on students in a tangible form for analysis and evaluation.

What is the Relationship Between Reflection and Professional Development?

Highly effective teachers are those who approach teaching as a craft, not a technology, and who are willing to try different approaches depending on a host of factors, most importantly, the subject matter and the group of students. Teaching as a craft requires a willingness by the teacher to observe teaching critically and to reflect upon how it can be continuously improved. As noted by some researchers, reflection is

> ...an approach to personal and organizational change and improvement that is open ended, that encourages us to continue learning and growing ourselves at the same time that it enhances the professional development of our students and colleagues and that holds tremendous potential for working out specific improvements in very different education organizations and contexts.[6]

Reflection is infinitely flexible and is not bound by a given profession, specialty area, or work environment. Its private nature permits critique without a sense of criticism and encourages growth without faultfinding.

It is through reflection that teachers are able to observe inconsistencies or discrepancies between what they hoped to accomplish in a lesson, assignment, or activity and what they did. It is this awareness of an incongruity between the ideal and reality that creates discomfort and an impetus for change.[7] Figure 5.1 contains the reflections of a music teacher who had just finished an impressive unit on multicultural music from Mexico, Kenya, and Japan. The lessons are activity-based and specific to curriculum standards.

Figure 5.1. Reflections on Multicultural Music Unit

In preparing for, and teaching, the lessons on multi-culturalism, I was both excited and anxious. At the conclusion of the ten-week unit, I felt that I needed to try a more hands-on approach (map making, group work, etc.) to identify geographical locations and discover cultural facts.

Based on this unit, I also recognized the need to develop and create a more objective and concise means of assessing student work. All of my assessments were heavily subjective.

Lastly, as a result of the time constrictions that rushed many lessons, I have discussed with my administrators the need for large blocks of time for projects such as this.

The desire to learn and grow suggested in this reflection is internally motivated by a drive for personal and professional achievement. The teacher was meeting external curriculum requirements but was modifying her practice (instructional strategies and assessment) around what she thought the students needed. For some, the change process remains a private conversation, and for others, it is benefited by external input and dialogue from respected colleagues and supervisors. No matter what the source or impetus, the need to grow and develop as a professional provides the trigger for improvement in a teacher's work with students.

How Does Reflection Contribute to Professional Development?

Portfolios provide an excellent tool to facilitate a process of reflection. Artifacts in the portfolio are a means to capture fleeting experiences or instructional moments for a more thoughtful and careful analysis. They "allow us to combine actual artifacts of teaching with a teacher's reflections enabling us to look beneath the surface of the performance itself and examine the decisions that shaped a teacher's actions."[8] Portfolios enhance the consideration of questions such as:

- What were the instructional goals?
- Did the activity match the goals?
- How did students respond to the activity?
- Were the learning goals achieved?
- What worked well?
- How could the activity be improved?

The process of analysis described above is one that begins during student teaching and hopefully continues throughout a teaching career. It is a "habit of inquiry" that many believe is fundamental for continuous professional growth.[9] Although most teachers associate professional supervision with a principal, self-evaluation and peer coaching have become more accepted as alternative methods for achieving similar goals.

Creating a more comprehensive performance portrait as described above entails calling on more than the principal or evaluator for input regarding performance. Figure 5.2 (p. 78) identifies key contributors to documenting teacher performance within a multifaceted data collection system that emphasizes portfolios.

Self-Reflection

First and foremost, the portfolio is a tool for self-reflection. Its development requires:

- a process of conceptualizing who the teacher is as a professional
- what the teacher believes is important
- how to capture the teacher's work in visual media
- how to use it for self-evaluation
- how to set goals that extend strengths and rectify weaknesses.

It is a self-directed exercise of understanding and defining what the teacher's professional actions mean. Every aspect of the portfolio reflects on the teacher as an individual and professional. The organization of the contents, the high-lighted professional work that is selected, and the personal commentary on what was learned provide a fuller, more holistic view of the teacher.

Self-reflection by teachers arises from a "personal need to understand, critique, and improve on their own practice."[10] A hallmark of "expert" versus "novice" teachers is their ability to learn from experience through observation

Figure 5.2. Prospective Contributors to a Teaching Portfolio

Contributor	*Roles*
Self	First and foremost, the teacher is the contributor to the performance portfolio. He or she knows what happens every day and can best offer evidence to support the accomplishment of key teaching responsibilities as well evidence of student learning success.
Students	Carefully constructed survey instruments, focusing on specific job behaviors and not on personality traits, can provide input from an important constituency.
Parents/Community Members	A teacher's performance portrait can be enhanced with communication to, and feedback from, parents or other community members. However, it is important to solicit feedback only on job-relevant performance that can be assessed by the parent or community member. For example, clarity of expectations for home support, promptness in keeping appointments, availability, and responsiveness might be useful feedback.
Peers	Depending on the teacher's role, peers can be called upon to provide insightful performance data. For example, team assignments, co-teaching, and similar responsibilities can be documented. However, as with other client groups, it is essential that peers provide feedback only on those teaching responsibilities for which the peer respondents have direct knowledge or observation.
Supervisor/Peer Evaluation Team	Unlike in most teacher evaluation systems, where the observation is the evaluation, in this model, the supervisor bases the evaluation on an analysis of the total evaluation portrait.

and reflection. Expert teachers continually adjust and modify instruction to maximize student learning. As a result, it is no surprise that research supports the essential nature of instructional self-assessment by effective, experienced teachers.[11] Experience without reflection does not improve instruction or teacher effectiveness. Rather, it is the combination of experience and thoughtful analysis that makes teachers more effective. As noted by one teacher educator:

> The ability to think about what one does and why—assessing past actions, current situations, and intended outcomes—is vital to intelligent practice, practice that is reflective rather than routine.[12]

Portfolios offer a unique vehicle for doing just this.

Research also suggests that the reflective process is further enhanced with the input of peers and supervisors.[13] Respected colleagues can provide a collaborative support network for the development of a portfolio, they can offer new and different insights on materials in the portfolio, or they can provide external information that becomes part of the portfolio. Some educators work collaboratively with others throughout the entire development process, providing each other with support and confirmation of their respective professional representations. They can offer advice on the organization of the portfolio, its contents, and professional goals.

The following suggestions offer ideas on how other educators can be involved in providing actual artifacts to be used in the portfolio, thus becoming part of the objective record upon which teachers can self-assess for growth.

Teaching Peers

There are a number of ways to include feedback from colleagues in the ongoing work of professional development. Inviting peers into the classroom, or asking peers who already work in the classroom (e.g., a resource/consulting teacher), can be a valuable source of feedback about performance. These colleagues can offer supportive, but honest, feedback about what, in their view, works well and can also offer suggestions for improvement. One way to collect peer feedback—and a method that can be included easily in a portfolio—is to use an observation form, either a structured one based on established instructional goals or an open-ended one to focus on teacher-specified concerns. The teacher can then react to the observations and suggestions with personal commentary on how she might use the information to enhance teaching.

Feedback from peers also can be collected with survey instruments. This approach is particularly useful when the teacher works closely with others in a team teaching situation or collaboratively with a number of teachers within a department. Figure 5.3 shows a sampling of possible survey items. It is important that the survey instrument focus on those professional responsibilities for which the peer respondents have some direct knowledge or observation.

Typically, when survey data are included in a portfolio, the results are summarized numerically and with narrative on the most noteworthy conclusions. However, individual survey instruments should not be included in the portfolio. Multiple examples of client surveys can be found in Appendix G.

Figure 5.3. Sample Items from a Peer Survey

Classroom Teacher Survey for Resource Teacher

Shares knowledge and information about new or improved methods of instruction.	YES	NO	NA

COMMENT: _____

_____

Communicates effectively with others and me regarding student progress.	YES	NO	NA

COMMENT: _____

_____

Enlists the support of other school personnel, parents, and community resources when necessary to meet the needs of students.	YES	NO	NA

COMMENT: _____

_____

Another effective means of soliciting peer feedback is to videotape a teaching episode and then ask colleagues to review it and offer suggestions for improvement. Although this strategy can provoke anxiety for the teacher, it is one of the most accurate means of recording instructional events aside from actual observation. An added benefit is that the video can be replayed repeatedly as observers analyze the activity or lesson for different purposes. As with real-time observations, peers can summarize the strengths and weaknesses of a recorded observation for inclusion in the portfolio along with the videotape and reflective commentary by the teacher.

Supervisors

Portfolios can provide the basis for a deeper, richer discussion of teacher strengths and weaknesses between the teacher and his or her supervisor than one based only on a supervisor's occasional classroom observation. When a portfolio consists of artifacts of performance related to instruction, student assessment, learning environment, and professional responsibilities, there is more substance for discussion. Moreover, when input from peers, students, perhaps parents and/or other individuals external to the school, and the teacher's self-reflection are included, we have a much clearer, deeper picture of performance and, thus, a stronger foundation upon which to plan professional development and to craft improvement plans for the teacher.

What Is the Format of a Portfolio for Professional Development?

When portfolios are used for evaluation or career advancement, their content tends to be more formally structured by predetermined or recommended performance criteria, but the organization of portfolios for professional development should be a reflection of the teacher and what he or she believes is important about teaching. The performance frameworks presented in Chapter 2 of this book closely reflect the literature on teaching and what most teachers consider to be important aspects of their work. Most frameworks include content knowledge, instruction, assessment, classroom management, and professionalism. Other approaches to organizing artifacts within the portfolio are more open-ended and context-based. Some teachers have organized their portfolios around an instructional question, such as "How can we motivate and encourage students to improve their performance in persuasive and expository writing?"[14] The range of possible organizational structures is shown in Figure 5.4.

Despite the range of possibilities in the overall organization of the portfolio, the greatest variation is seen in the selection and presentation of artifacts within a given portfolio. As one set of authors advocated:

> Because professional teaching portfolios serve as visual representations of teachers, their contents should be determined by individual teachers and should vary significantly, depending on each teacher's philosophy, values, and viewpoints as well as on teaching and collegiate experience.[15]

The kinds of activities, lessons, experiences, and accomplishments exhibited by teachers will provide a vivid representation of who they are as professionals and what they believe is important about teaching and learning. Similar types of artifacts (e.g., lesson/unit plans, student work) can be used for both evaluation and professional development. An array of possible artifacts for inclusion in the portfolio are described in Chapter 2 and listed in various appendices. In

Figure 5.4. Continuum of
Organizational Frameworks for Portfolios

More traditional	$\Rightarrow \Rightarrow \Rightarrow \Rightarrow \Rightarrow$	*Less traditional*
Interstate New Teacher Assessment and Support Consortium Standards (INTASC)[16]	Douglas County Outstanding Teacher Program[17]	Literacy Artifacts and Themes[18]
◆ Knowledge of subject	◆ Assessment and instruction	◆ Myself as a reader
◆ Learning and human development	◆ Content and pedagogy	◆ Myself as a writer
◆ Adapting instruction	◆ Collaboration and partnership	◆ Myself as a listener
◆ Strategies		◆ Myself as a speaker
◆ Motivation and management		◆ Myself as a teacher/learner
◆ Communication skills		◆ Myself as a monitor/assessor
◆ Planning		◆ Myself as a community member
◆ Assessment		
◆ Commitment		
◆ Partnerships		

addition to these items, the following materials might be considered for purposes of professional development:

- ◆ Résumé
- ◆ Statement of educational philosophy
- ◆ Professional goal statement/growth plan
- ◆ Evaluations by supervisors or colleagues
- ◆ Photographs and visual documentation
- ◆ Student and parent feedback
- ◆ Descriptions of original ideas for use in the classroom or school
- ◆ Inspirational items such as quotes or pictures
- ◆ Personal reflections.[19]

The critical difference in portfolios used primarily for professional development is in the selection of specific items for inclusion. When a teacher is trying to promote or document professional growth, there should be evidence of change and improvement over time. This means including less stellar work along with the new and better versions of the lesson, assessment, or instructional strategy. In describing this shift in thinking, one teacher observed:

> Cynthia and I had spent a lot of time trying to *prove* something about ourselves as teachers rather than working to *improve* our methods of instruction. We had left out the materials that showed what we had learned about our own instruction and the impact of that instruction on student work. [emphasis in the original][20]

Professional development involves the examination and improvement of weaknesses, not just the showcasing of strengths.

How Can Reflections Add Value to Portfolios?

Whereas captions attached to portfolio artifacts may be thought of as road signs, reflections within the context of teacher portfolios may be thought of as travel guides. Reflections by a teacher are extended, thoughtful analyses of certain artifacts included in a portfolio and the role that these artifacts play in the teacher's performance. The teacher portfolio has been defined as "an individualized portrait of the teacher as a professional, *reflecting on* his or her philosophy and practice" (emphasis added).[21] Another description holds that a portfolio is "a powerful means for the articulation of *thoughtful practice*" (emphasis added).[22] Even more bluntly, a portfolio without reflection has been characterized as "little more than an exercise in amassing papers."[23] In short, reflecting upon one's work through the choices of artifacts included in one's portfolio is integral to the value of portfolios in the professional development and growth of a teacher. Whether recognizing areas of ample evidence or identifying areas that are less strong or even weak, a teacher who is reflecting upon artifacts of his or her own practice is engaged in sustained self-reflection, self-evaluation, and growth.

Reflections in a portfolio can take several forms. They may be a paragraph to several pages in length per artifact. Or a single reflective piece may draw upon, and refer to, several artifacts contained within a portfolio, essentially unifying them to illustrate a particular practice in the classroom. For instance, teachers may reflect upon the integration of resources that are used for planning, choices made concerning instructional activities, and the role of an assessment piece in a particular unit. Though several discrete teaching responsibilities are documented by the individual artifacts, the teacher's written refection integrates those artifacts and responsibilities to demonstrate the complex strata of teaching.

It should be noted that reflection pieces are longer and more involved than descriptions that may be included in a caption. Captions, as described in Chapter 2, are intended to assist a reviewer in understanding the context and purpose of an artifact. Reflections are intended to capture a *teacher's* understanding and judgment of the value and effectiveness of a particular artifact.

As with captions, reflections may be standardized by a school or district, or discretion may by left to the individual teacher as to how to construct reflective pieces. For example, a school district may require teachers to articulate their philosophy of education, describe their classroom management strategies, or explain their rationale for sequencing their curriculum. Such reflections may be limited in length and even format. For instance, teachers may be required to write no more than a single, typed page, thereby requiring very focused reflection and limiting the amount of time necessary for the teacher to write and for the reviewer to read.

Reflective Journals

On the other hand, reflections may take a far more involved role in a teacher portfolio. Reflective journals require a series of reflections on teacher performance over an extended period of time.[24] A journal may be required to draw together all of the artifacts within a single portfolio. Or a reflective journal may be kept over a designated time period, in essence serving as a diary of teaching. The reflective journal then becomes another document within a portfolio, harnessing the power of writing in personal and professional development. However, it also involves considerable time, which may not be an abundant resource in the lives of most teachers.

Reflective Prompts

One strategy for making reflections both feasible and meaningful is to use reflective prompts. Reflective prompts are specific statements or questions provided by a school or school district for teachers to respond to within their portfolios. Reflective prompts engage teachers in the analysis of their practice and its impact on students. Figure 5.5 contains four sources of reflective prompts and some specific examples from each of these sources. Whether universal in nature, linked to a particular unit of study, driven by school or district goals, or evolved from a teacher's own professional development plan, reflective prompts serve to focus a teacher's self-evaluation and professional introspection.

Figure 5.5. Sources and Examples of Reflective Prompts

Universal Prompts[25]

♦ What is my philosophy of learning?

♦ How do I define my role as a teacher?

♦ How do I teach?

♦ What feedback have I received from students, parents, colleagues, and supervisors?

♦ What have I learned?

♦ What standards do I value most for my students?

♦ What outcomes do I expect of my students, what have I done to get them there, and how will I know that they have been successful?

♦ What does the range of performance look like in my classroom, what possible reasons are there, and how can discrepancies be addressed?

Unit-Specific Prompts[26]

♦ What makes this unit worthwhile to teach and study?

♦ How and why have I organized the unit for instruction?

♦ What have I done to make instruction interesting, accessible, and effective?

♦ What gains or changes should I see in students as a result of this instruction, and how will I know it?

♦ What is the context of this unit?

♦ How and why have I selected the resources that I have used with this unit?

♦ What was successful about this unit?

♦ What about this unit would I change?

Prompts Based on School/District Goals

♦ Achievement goal: What specific instruction have I provided to improve student performance on the _____ standardized test of achievement and what have been the effects?

♦ Equity goal: What subgroups within my class are achieving below expectations and how have I attempted to reduce this disparity and with what effects?

♦ Partnership goal: What strategies have I used to involve parents in their student's learning in my class and what have been the effects?

Prompts Based on Individual Goals

Individual goals may be developed in isolation by a teacher, in partnership with a team or department, or in collaboration with a supervisor. Obviously, individual goals are highly idiosyncratic. The following examples only illustrate some possibilities:

♦ How has my use of manipulatives to teach fractions affected the learning of students?

♦ How has my use of a portfolio writing process affected students' writing skills?

♦ How has my integration of the internet as a source for student's science projects affected the quality of their research?

How Do Educators Perceive the Use of Portfolios for Professional Development?

We have worked with a number of school systems in implementing professional portfolios. In one school system, we conducted a detailed study on the effects of portfolio use and found positive perceptions about their use in the evaluation process and their contribution to professional growth. (See "Materials for Evaluating the Use of Teacher Portfolios" in Appendix C and on the companion CD for various instruments that can be used to evaluate the use of portfolios. Examples include open-ended surveys, structured questionnaires with rating scales, and focus group questions.)

A sample of key questions from the structured questionnaire data that we collected is summarized in Figure 5.6. Findings indicated that teachers and administrators were positive about the self-reflection that portfolio development encouraged and its assistance in identifying areas of strength and weakness. Teachers, however, did voice concerns about the time required to develop the portfolio. It is important to note that this questionnaire was administered only one year after the introduction of portfolios as part of a comprehensive evaluation system. With further training and the assimilation of portfolios into the existing culture of the schools, we're optimistic that this concern will be allayed.

Figure 5.6. Sample of Structured Questionnaire Data

Rating Scale: 1 = Strongly Disagree and 4 = Strongly Agree

Statement	Teachers (N=310)	Administrators (N=15)
The portfolio promotes two-way communication between my administrator and me.	2.54	3.40
Development of a portfolio encourages self-reflection about my work.	2.74	3.07
Development of a portfolio assists me in identifying areas of strength and weakness.	2.58	2.79
The time required of me to develop a portfolio is reasonable.	2.09	2.67
The portfolio offers additional substance for discussion at the evaluation review conferences.	2.74	3.27

In addition to the collection of survey data, we ran focus groups of both administrators and teachers. Administrators were enthusiastic about almost every aspect of portfolio use. Despite the time demands of reviewing portfolios, they regarded them as extremely helpful in illuminating the comprehensive nature and depth of their teachers' work. Administrators felt they "knew" their teachers far better after looking at their portfolios, and this knowledge significantly contributed to the substance of year-end conferences. Focus group discussions with teachers, however, revealed some ambivalence similar to that reflected in the survey data. Representative of some teachers, one said, "It's hard to make the portfolio a priority with all the other things teachers must do." In positive contrast, another said, "[The portfolio] helps me know where I need and want to go. It keeps me from becoming stagnant." Clearly, this small study shows that there is tremendous potential for positive outcomes with the use of portfolios, but the time required to construct it remains as a concern in their wide scale use.

Summary

As is the case for many other educational reforms, it is crucial to develop a support structure for the development of portfolios and the self-reflective process. There must be encouragement through a school-wide initiative to make portfolios and self-reflection an integral part of the culture, to assist in the development process, to provide adequate resources, and to safeguard and protect teachers from unfair use of their reflections.[27] Trust is fundamental to the professional growth process. To grow and stretch professionally, especially in collegial exchanges, teachers must feel safe and supported in their efforts.

The use of portfolios for professional development has been shown to have tremendous benefit for some teachers despite concerns, especially regarding the time required to construct them. Beginning teachers as well as veterans have found that portfolios offer a new perspective on their work, giving it meaning and value. Moreover, the work of the National School Reform Faculty has revealed the importance of coupling portfolio development with collegial review and structured critique. Their experiences suggest the additional benefits listed below.

- ◆ Stimulates fundamental changes in teaching practices.
- ◆ Shifts the responsibility for professional accountability from administrators to teachers.
- ◆ Focuses attention on how teachers think about their work.
- ◆ Enables the teacher to wrestle with the important questions in their respective discipline.
- ◆ Fosters enlightenment, not simply evaluation.
- ◆ Sharpens the inquiry skills of every participant in the review process.[28]

Under the right conditions, portfolios offer a powerful tool to facilitate self-assessment and thoughtful reflection on a teacher's current practice and how to improve and grow professionally. It is an infinitely flexible tool that offers a viable alternative to traditional supervision and can be adapted to an array of contexts with a wide range of professionals. Ultimately, it enables each teacher to construct his or her own knowledge about teaching and to take control of his or her development as a professional.

References

1. Cushman, K. (1999). Educators making portfolios: First results from the national school reform faculty. *Phi Delta Kappan, 80*(10), 744–750.

2. Cushman, K. (1999), p. 745.

3. Cushman, K. (1999), p. 749.

4. See Wolfe-Quintero, K., & Brown, J.D. (1998). Teacher portfolios. *TESOL Journal, 7*(6), 24–27; Collins, A. (1991). Portfolios for biology teacher assessment. *Journal of Personnel Evaluation in Education, 5,* 147–167; Rousculp, E.E., & Maring, G.H. (1992). Portfolios for a community of learners. *Journal of Reading, 35*(5), 378–385.

5. Anderson, R. S., & DeMeulle, L. (1998). Portfolio use in twenty-four teacher education programs. *Teacher Education Quarterly, 25,* 23–31.

6. Osterman, K. F., & Kottkamp, R. B. (1993). *Reflective practice for educators: Improving schooling through professional development.* Newbury Park, CA: Corwin Press.

7. Osterman, K. F., & Kottkamp, R. B. (1993).

8. Stone, B. A. (1998). Problems, pitfalls, and benefits of portfolios. *Teacher Education Quarterly, 25*(1), 105–114, p. 106.

9. Lyons, N. (1999). How portfolios can shape emerging practice. *Educational Leadership, 56*(8), 63–65.

10. Airasion, P. W., & Gullickson, A. (1997). Teacher self-evaluation. In J. H. Stronge (Ed.), *Evaluating teaching: A guide to current thinking and best practice* (215–247). Thousand Oaks, CA: Corwin Press, p. 215.

11. Covino, E. A., & Iwanicki, E. F. (1996). Experienced teachers: Their constructs of effective teaching. *Journal of Personnel Evaluation in Education, 10,* 325–363.

12. Richert, A. E. (1990). Teaching teachers to reflect: A consideration of programme structure. *Journal of Curriculum Studies, 22,* 509–527, p. 525.

13. Good, T. L., & Brophy, J. E. (1987). *Looking in classrooms.* New York: Harper & Row; Duke, D. L., & Stiggins, R. J. (1985). *Five keys to growth through teacher evaluation.* Portland, OR: Northwest Regional Educational Laboratory.

14. Van Wagenen, L., & Hibbard, K. M. (1998). Building teacher portfolios. *Educational Leadership, 55*(5), 26–29, p. 28.

15. Hurst, B., Wilson, C., & Cramer, G. (1998). Professional teaching portfolios: Tools for reflection, growth, and advancement. *Phi Delta Kappan, 78*(8), 578–582, p. 579.

16. Campbell, D. M., Cignetti, P. B., Melenyzer, B.J., Nettles, D. H., & Wyman, R. M., Jr. (1997). *How to develop a professional portfolio: A manual for teachers.* Needham Heights, MA: Allyn & Bacon.

17. Wolf, K., Lichtenstein, G., Bartlett, E., & Hartman, D. (1996). Professional development and teaching portfolios: The Douglas County Outstanding Teacher Program. *Journal of Personnel Evaluation in Education, 10,* 279–286.

18. Rogers, S.E., & Danielson, K. E. (1996). *Teacher portfolios: Literacy artifacts and themes.* Portsmouth, NH: Heinemann.

19. See Hurst, B., Wilson, C., & Cramer, G. (1998); Wolf, K., Lichtenstein, G., Bartlett, E., & Hartman, D. (1996); Wolfe-Quintero, K., & Brown, J. D. (1998).

20. Van Wagenen, L., & Hibbard, K. M. (1998). Building teacher portfolios. *Educational Leadership, 55*(5), 26–29, p. 27.

21. Painter, B. (2001). Using teacher portfolios. *Educational Leadership, 58* (5), 31–34, p. 31.

22. Martin-Kneip, G. O. (1999). *Capturing the wisdom of practice.* Alexandria, VA: Association for Supervision and Curriculum Development, p. 83.

23. Wolf, K. (1999), p. 6.

24. Yoo, S. Y. (2001). Using portfolios to reflect on practice. *Educational Leadership, 58*(8), 78–81, p. 78.

25. Adapted in part from Martin-Kneip, G. O. (1999) and Perkins, P. G., & Gelfer, J. I. (1998). Producing teacher/staff portfolios: A method for effective evaluation. *Catalyst for Change, 28*(1), 17–20, pp. 18–19.

26. Adapted from Collins, A. (1991). Portfolios for biology teacher assessment. *Journal of Personnel Evaluation in Education, 5,* 147–167; and Wolf, K. (1999). *Leading the professional portfolio process for change.* Arlington Heights, IL: Skylight.

27. Airasion, P. W., & Gullickson, A. (1997).

28. Cushman, K. (1999).

6

THE ROLE OF PORTFOLIOS FOR THE TEACHING PROFESSION

You must be the change you wish to see in the world.
Mahatma Gandhi

Change must begin with ourselves, and the portfolio offers one means of gaining some perspective on our work to inform that change. We discuss both the advantages and disadvantages in the use of portfolios for teacher evaluation and professional development throughout the chapters in this book. As with any tool, both the context in which the portfolio is used, and how individual teachers implement it, will vary. These variations in implementation will affect the portfolio's utility and meaningfulness. It is our intent to suggest structures and processes that optimize the portfolio's benefits and minimize its drawbacks in most situations. Given the personal nature of portfolios, however, it is imperative that design and implementation questions be examined and resolved.

To assist teachers, schools, and districts as they consider the use of portfolios, it is useful to summarize what we have learned about them and discuss the future possibilities for portfolios. In this final chapter, we address these questions:

- ◆ What have we learned?
- ◆ Where do we go from here?

What Have We Learned?

Based on our accumulated experience with teacher portfolios, we have learned that they provide an unparalleled depth of understanding regarding a teacher's practice, along with incredible flexibility in their organization and purpose. Portfolios can be used for hiring, evaluation, professional development, license renewal, performance bonuses, and advanced certification. Portfolios are teacher-directed because teachers determine what to include in the portfolio, even with an externally imposed framework that is highly prescriptive. Teachers choose the content and the format of entries. As a result, the portfolio reflects the circumstances specific to an individual teacher as well as his or her unique view of teaching. Figure 6.1 summarizes many of the benefits of portfolios with regard to the two areas of our focus: evaluation and professional development.

Potential for Use

Although portfolios can be used for a variety of purposes, many of them can be viewed as either evaluative or developmental. For evaluative purposes, the emphasis in portfolio development is on documenting performance through the selection of carefully coordinated artifacts that reflect all facets of teaching including planning, instruction, assessment, classroom management, and professionalism. The portfolio is able to accommodate the complexities of teaching at different grade levels, in different settings, and for different subject areas. This approach to evaluation recognizes the autonomy of individual teachers and shifts from others, such as principals, to teachers the responsibility for the documentation of performance.

The greater potential for portfolios, however, possibly lies in their use for professional development either in conjunction with evaluation or as a separate activity. Portfolios provide an opportunity to "freeze" teaching moments and extract them from the daily routine of teaching for closer examination and analysis. Through thoughtful reflection, teachers become more aware of their assumptions about learning and their instructional effectiveness. Awareness of practice and how to improve it are considered prerequisites for the capacity to grow professionally.[1] The portfolio is an ideal vehicle for facilitating the development of awareness about teaching and thus enhancing the capacity of the teacher to grow professionally, especially when it is reviewed and discussed with supervisors or colleagues. Through a process of analysis, reflection, and dialogue with others, areas for future development can be identified. The portfolio, then, becomes a tool to chronicle efforts to modify practices, materials, or ways of thinking about a particular instructional concern over time.

Pitfalls of Use

Despite the many advantages of portfolios for a whole range of purposes, there are a few drawbacks to their use. One of the most frequently cited concerns is the amount of time required for their construction by the teacher and review by administrators or colleagues.[2] Some teachers complain that they take valuable time away from planning and instruction. In addition, portfolios can

Figure 6.1. Benefits in Using Teacher Portfolios[3]

Primary Benefits	Examples	Related to Evaluation	Related to Professional Development
Fosters self-reflection	◆ Makes teachers more aware of their strengths and weaknesses ◆ Helps teachers advance their own practice		✔
Enhances teacher efficacy	◆ Treats teachers as professionals ◆ Improves teacher morale and motivation ◆ Encourages teachers to represent their own knowledge and skills	✔	✔
Encourages collaboration	◆ Provides opportunities for collegial teacher activities—e.g., action research ◆ Encourages collegial interactions and discussions about teaching		✔
Enhances process of evaluation	◆ Gives teachers an active role in assessing performance, not a passive one ◆ Gives teachers a voice in shaping their own assessment and improvement	✔	
Promotes change	◆ Changes practice through personal development, not top-down mandates ◆ Encourages replacing unproductive instructional practices ◆ Recognizes that organizational change is usually the result of individuals changing themselves	✔	✔
Encourages teacher and school improvement	◆ Encourages ongoing teacher development ◆ Focuses improvement at the classroom or school level	✔	✔

be viewed as messy to construct, cumbersome, difficult to assess, and possibly misleading in terms of a teacher's abilities.[4] This last concern is particularly problematic, and caution must be taken not to focus on quantity over quality, or presentation skills over teaching skills and student learning results, especially when the purpose is evaluative. Figure 6.2 summarizes these potential pitfalls.

Figure 6.2. Possible Liabilities in Using Teacher Portfolios[5]

Primary Liabilities	Examples	Related to Evaluation	Related to Professional Development
Time consuming	♦ Costly in terms of teacher time to maintain ♦ Costly in terms of administrator time to evaluate	✔	✔
Detract from teaching	♦ Construction can take time away from teaching and other responsibilities		✔
Inaccurate picture of performance	♦ Potential to reflect presentation rather than teaching skills ♦ Possible emphasis on quantity over quality ♦ Vulnerable to misrepresentations	✔	

Although we acknowledge the unavoidable fact that the development of a portfolio takes time, we believe it is time well spent when it improves the practice of teaching. Because the contents of a portfolio should be a carefully selected sampling of *existing* materials for teaching, not newly created ones, it is the reflection upon those artifacts that takes time. Reflection, like other types of learning, requires a personal investment to reap the rewards of better performance.

Where Do We Go From Here?

With our current understanding of the possible functions and formats for portfolios, we believe their future is very promising. Portfolios have captured the imagination of both teachers and those who must make evaluative decisions, such as principals, because they provide a bridge between the goals of these two groups. Unlike traditional evaluation, the development of portfolios can be a meaningful experience for the teacher and it can offer evaluators an incomparable window on the practice of a teacher. Portfolios supplement other methods of evaluation, primarily observation, and, taken together, they can provide a "union of insufficiencies, a marriage of complements, in which the flaws of individual approaches to assessment are offset by the virtues of their fellows."[6]

Multiple Purposes

We believe that portfolios can serve the dual goals of evaluation and professional development and that these goals actually complement each other as proposed above. We suggest, like others, that the two goals are "part of an interconnected process, not isolated elements"[7] and that they make the experience more productive. We are concerned, however, that mandating the use of portfolios for either purpose without the proper support and conditions could undermine their effectiveness, especially for evaluation. Teachers need guidance and training to comfortably begin the collection and selection process. Alternatives to full-scale mandatory implementation include:

- using the portfolio to mentor new teachers
- giving experienced teachers an opportunity to substitute the portfolio for the formal observation and evaluation process
- requiring the portfolio to achieve outstanding or master teacher status

Best Practice for Implementation

Based on our collective experience with portfolios over the last fifteen years, there is a clearer understanding of how best to design and implement portfolios. There have been failures. For example, early efforts in Tennessee and Florida with portfolios failed as a result of inadequate guidance regarding the portfolio contents and a lack of local support in promoting a reflective approach to the process.[8] We now can be more definitive about the recommended portfolio contents and implementation features. For example, it is clear that collections of documents are meaningless without captions to explain the reason for their inclusion and reflective commentaries to explain how the various documents fit together.

Advancement of the Profession

Ultimately, portfolios offer a means to define teaching as a profession. This was one of the original goals of the National Board for Professional Teaching Standards. "Portfolios allow us...to look beneath the surface of the performance itself and examine the decisions that shaped a teacher's actions."[9] It is this very act of self-analysis of the decision-making processes that defines a professional. By articulating the standards of our practice and assessing the decision making of our members, we take important steps toward professionalizing education. Thus, portfolios serve not only the advancement of teachers and their schools, but also the profession as a whole.

Need for Research

Many of the drawbacks to portfolios can be addressed through more specific design guidelines and formative support within the local context. One major concern, however, remains the lack of research on the technical aspects of portfolios, such as validity and reliability. In 1994, a researcher noted that the "enthusiasm for both student and teacher portfolios might presently be outpacing the evidence for their efficacy as assessment tools."[10] This observation continues to be true today with the notable exception of the construct and consequential validity study of the National Board certification system.[11] More rigorous research of this type is needed to confirm the glowing accolades of teachers, teacher educators, and assessment experts.

We recommend that you consider the following important questions, presented in Figure 6.3, as you strive for the optimal use of portfolios.

Because of its flexibility, the portfolio is a tool that can serve multiple functions like licensure and hiring; it can also be used to encourage an array of professionally valued activities like reflection, collaboration, mentoring, action research, and continuous improvement. As educators, many of us recognize the importance of these activities, yet acknowledge the scarcity of opportunities to engage in them. The extent to which portfolios can foster communities of learners at the local, state, or national level around these activities will be the ultimate measure of their value.

Summary

As we hope is now evident, portfolios can be a powerful tool for documenting professional endeavors and examining them. They can portray both the "what" and "why" of instruction. They can provide a forum for sharing examples of your teaching and for understanding about one's teaching. If portfolios are developed with a clear purpose, as we suggest throughout this book, they should tell a story or paint a picture about someone's performance, results, and values as a teacher. Portfolios have the potential to change the way teaching is defined, assessed, and valued in society.[12] It is up to us who use and advocate the use of portfolios to realize that potential.

Figure 6.3. Guiding Questions for the Use of Portfolios

Consideration	Guiding Questions
Purpose	*What is the purpose of the portfolio?* ♦ The purpose will influence the organizing framework for the portfolio, its contents, and the nature of the reflections. ♦ The context in which the portfolios are constructed will also influence how teachers approach the task, and this context should mirror and support the stated purposes.
Expectations	*Have clear expectations for the organization and implementation of the portfolio been established?* ♦ Well-articulated standards of teaching and clear design guidelines will elevate the portfolio from the "great paper chase" to a professional exercise in self-analysis and renewal.
Reflection	*Has reflection been built into the preparation of portfolios?* ♦ For portfolios to represent a teacher and his or her work, there must be clearly defined reasons and explanations for the inclusion of materials. ♦ It is the reflective process of construction that differentiates a portfolio from a scrapbook. ♦ The use of both captions for individual artifacts, and longer reflective commentary on subsections or the entire portfolio, are critical in maximizing the value of portfolios.
Training	*Has training been provided for all parties involved in the use of portfolios?* ♦ The responsibility for portfolio development falls on the teacher and is highly dependent on his or her individual capacity to make sense or meaning of his or her work with students. ♦ Teachers will need training in the processes of collection, selection, and reflection[13] for portfolio preparation. ♦ The professional development associated with portfolios is not only a product of the process, but also must be part of the process.
Collaboration	*Is collaboration encouraged in the development and analysis of the portfolio?* ♦ Construction of a portfolio is a creative process and is enhanced by feedback from others on its contents and the story it tells. ♦ Dialogue with peers and mentors helps the teacher to clarify the original intent or purpose of including certain objects, what they reveal about strengths and weaknesses, and directions for further development. ♦ Teachers must be well supported in this professional growth effort.

References

1. Duke, D. L. (1990). Developing teacher evaluation systems that promote professional growth. *Journal of Personnel Evaluation in Education, 4,* 131–144; Osterman, K. F., & Kottkamp, R. B. (1993). *Reflective practice for educators: Improving schooling through professional development.* Newbury Park, CA: Corwin Press.

2. Stone, B.A. (1998). Problems, pitfalls, and benefits of portfolios. *Teacher Education Quarterly, 25*(1), 105–114.

3. Portions adapted from Airasian, P. W., & Gullickson, A. (1997). Teacher self-evaluation. In J. H. Stronge (Ed.), *Evaluating teaching: A guide to current thinking and best practices* (pp 215–247). Thousand Oaks, CA: Corwin Press.

4. Wolf, K. (1991). The schoolteacher's portfolio: Issues in design, implementation, and evaluation. *Phi Delta Kappan 73,* 129–136.

5. Portions adapted from Wolf, K. (1991).

6. Shulman, L. S. (1988). A union of insufficiencies: Strategies for teacher assessment in a period of reform. *Educational Leadership, 46*(3), 36–41, p. 38.

7. Lyons, N. P. (1996). A grassroots experiment in performance assessment. *Educational Leadership, 53*(6), 64–67, p. 66.

8. Shulman, L. S. (1988).

9. Stone, B.A. (1998).

10. Wolf, K. (1994). Teaching portfolios: Capturing the complexities of teaching. In L.I. Ingvarson & R. Chadbourne (Eds.), *Valuing teachers' work: New directions in teacher appraisal* (pp. 112–136). Victoria, Australia: The Australian Council for Educational Research, p. 113.

11. Bond, L., Smith, T., Baker, W. K., & Hattie, J. A. (2000). *The certification system of the National Board for Professional Teaching Standards: A construct and consequential validity study.* Greensboro, NC: Center for Educational Research and Evaluation, The University of North Carolina at Greensboro.

12. Zubizarreta, J. (1994). Teaching portfolios and the beginning teacher. *Phi Delta Kappan, 76*(3), 323–326.

13. Pearlman, M. (1997, March). *Designing in validity: The National Board for Professional Teaching Standards certification assessments.* Paper presented at the annual conference of the American Educational Research Association, Chicago, IL.

Appendices

HOW THE APPENDICES CAN BE USED

The materials in the appendices provide a framework for a more traditionally organized portfolio based on commonly agreed upon expectations for teachers. These expectations not only underlie most evaluation systems used by school districts but also they reflect what most teachers would want to consider in the creation of a portfolio for their own professional development. The following summarizes the possible questions you might have about the use of portfolios with the corresponding section in the appendices that offers guidance in answering the question. Electronic versions of these materials can be found on the companion CD.

Where to Find Answers to Your Questions in the Appendices

Question	Possible Answer(s) Contained in the Appendices	Appendix
How can teaching be defined for documentation in a portfolio?	◆ Performance Standards	A
How can different levels of performance be distinguished based on the portfolio?	◆ Performance Assessment Rubrics	B
How do I organize my portfolio?	◆ General Guidelines for Organizing a Teacher Portfolio	C
How can I document specific teaching responsibilities?	◆ Performance Standards Cross-Referenced with Sample Artifacts	D
	◆ Sample Artifacts Cross-Referenced with Performance Standards	E

Question	Possible Answer(s) Contained in the Appendices	Appendix
How can supervisors/evaluators provide feedback on portfolio contents?	◆ Portfolio Feedback Form	F
How can feedback from clients be included in the portfolio?	◆ Client Surveys	G
How could a school system introduce portfolios and persuade teachers to use them as part of an evaluation system?	◆ Public Dissemination Plan	H
	◆ Sample Newsletters Introducing the Concept of Portfolios	I
How could the district-wide use of portfolios be evaluated?	◆ Materials for Evaluating the Use of Teacher Portfolios	J

The appendices begin with suggested Performance Standards that are intended to define the structure for the portfolio, with subsequent materials providing tools for the development of portfolio contents and implementation at the district level. Most of the appendices are self-explanatory or include a description for their use.

Appendix A

PERFORMANCE STANDARDS

Description of Performance Standards

The foundation of a teacher evaluation system is the use of clearly described responsibilities for teachers. A fair and comprehensive evaluation system should provide sufficient detail and accuracy so that educators and their supervisors can reasonably understand the job expectations.

The expectations for teacher performance used in this book are defined using a three-tiered description of:

- ◆ Domains of Performance,
  - ◆ Performance Standards,
    - ◆ Performance Indicators.

Domains of Performance

There are four general Domains of Performance for teachers. Domains of Performance reflect the framework for describing major aspects of the work of teachers.

1. *Instructional Skills.* This domain of performance encompasses both organizing for instruction and delivery of instruction. The major responsibilities include planning and implementing a variety of activities consistent with instructional objectives, and selecting instructional methods compatible with student abilities and learning styles.

2. *Assessment Skills.* This domain includes the responsibilities for conducting evaluation and providing feedback to students that encourages student progress and measures student achievement.

3. *Learning Environment Skills.* The learning environment skills domain includes the teacher's responsibilities for planning and dem-

onstrating effective routines and procedures that create an organized and positive learning environment.

4. *Professionalism.* This final domain defines the responsibilities for demonstrating a commitment to professional ethics and growth and for complying with district policies and procedures.

Performance Standards

Performance Standards are the fundamental duties or responsibilities of a teacher. They are organized into the four general "Domains of Performance" identified above. For teachers, there are 18 Performance Standards. An example of a Performance Standard is listed below:

Performance Standard I-1: The teacher demonstrates current and accurate knowledge of subject matter covered in the curriculum.

A full listing of teacher Performance Standards is provided in the following pages.

Performance Indicators

Performance Indicators are used in the evaluation system to do just what the term implies, they indicate, in observable behaviors, performance of the major responsibilities. The sample performance indicators provided for each responsibility in the following section are not intended to be exhaustive lists, nor are they meant to be prescriptive. The following is an example of the performance indicators for *Performance Standard I-1:*

Performance Standard I-1: The teacher demonstrates current and accurate knowledge of subject matter covered in the curriculum.

Sample Performance Indicators:

   a. The teacher exhibits an understanding of the subject areas taught.

   b. The teacher demonstrates skills relevant to the subject area.

   c. The teacher utilizes a variety of resources in the subject area.

   d. The teacher demonstrates an ability to make topics and activities meaningful and relevant to each student.

   e. The teacher exhibits/demonstrates an understanding of technology skills appropriate for grade level/subject matter.

Yourtown Public Schools
Teacher Performance Standards

Domain I: Instructional Skills

Organizing for Instruction

Performance Standard **I-1**   **The teacher demonstrates current and accurate knowledge of subject matter covered in the curriculum.**

Sample Performance Indicators:

a. The teacher exhibits an understanding of the subject areas taught.

b. The teacher demonstrates skills relevant to the subject area.

c. The teacher utilizes a variety of resources in the subject area.

d. The teacher demonstrates an ability to make topics and activities meaningful and relevant to each student.

e. The teacher exhibits/demonstrates an understanding of technology skills appropriate for grade level/subject matter.

Performance Standard **I-2**   **The teacher plans instruction to achieve desired student learning objectives that reflect current district curriculum.**

Sample Performance Indicators:

a. The teacher selects student objectives for lessons consistent with district guidelines and curriculum.

b. The teacher selects learning activities for lessons consistent with district curriculum and student needs.

c. The teacher develops lesson plans that are clear, logical, and sequential.

d. The teacher plans purposeful assignments for teacher assistants, substitute teachers, student teachers, and others.

Performance Standard **I-3**   **The teacher uses materials and resources compatible with students' needs and abilities that support the current district curriculum.**

Sample Performance Indicators:

a.   The teacher selects a variety of materials and media that support the curriculum.

b.   The teacher integrates available technology into the curriculum.

c.   The teacher selects materials and media that match learning styles of individual students.

d.   The teacher ensures that materials and media are appropriate and challenging for instructional levels.

e.   The teacher uses materials, media, and equipment that motivate students to learn.

Performance Standard **I-4**   **The teacher links present content/skills with past and future learning experiences, other subject areas, and real world experiences/ applications.**

Sample Performance Indicators:

a.   The teacher links current objectives of learning to prior student learning.

b.   The teacher solicits comments, questions, examples, demonstrations, or other contributions from students throughout the lesson.

c.   The teacher matches the content/skills taught with the overall scope and sequence of the curriculum.

Delivery of Instruction

Performance Standard **I-5**   **The teacher communicates effectively with students and models standard English.**

Sample Performance Indicators:

a.   The teacher uses standard English grammar when communicating with students.

b.   The teacher uses precise language, acceptable oral expression, and written communication.

c. The teacher explains concepts and lesson content to students in a logical and sequential manner.

d. The teacher emphasizes major points of concerns by using techniques such as repetition and verbal or non-verbal clues.

e. The teacher actively listens and responds in a constructive manner.

Performance Standard **I-6** **The teacher uses a variety of instructional strategies that promote student learning.**

Sample Performance Indicators:

a. The teacher monitors student understanding and paces the lesson based on achievement.

b. The teacher uses a variety of instructional strategies to encourage student achievement.

c. The teacher uses questioning strategies to engage students and promote learning.

d. The teacher effectively implements a variety of learning activities and experiences consistent with instructional objectives.

e. The teacher maximizes student learning by providing opportunities to participate actively and successfully.

f. The teacher provides guided and independent practice of skills.

g. The teacher summarizes and reviews major concepts from the lesson.

h. The teacher provides evidence of measurable student progress.

Performance Standard **I-7** **The teacher provides learning opportunities for individual differences.**

Sample Performance Indicators:

a. The teacher identifies and plans for the instructional needs for all students and provides remedial and enrichment activities as necessary.

b. The teacher explains content and demonstrates skills in a variety of ways to meet the needs of each student.

c. The teacher gives each student an equal opportunity for involvement in learning.

d. The teacher holds each student individually responsible for learning.

Domain A: Assessment Skills

Performance Standard **A-1**   **The teacher provides a variety of ongoing and culminating assessments to measure student performance.**

Sample Performance Indicators:

a. The teacher effectively uses both teacher-made and standardized tests to measure student performance.

b. The teacher uses oral, nonverbal, and written forms of assessment to measure student performance.

c. The teacher uses authentic assessment to measure student performance.

d. The teacher uses available data sources to examine and document student progress.

Performance Standard **A-2**   **The teacher provides ongoing and timely feedback to encourage student progress.**

Sample Performance Indicators:

a. The teacher monitors student progress before, during, and after instruction.

b. The teacher provides feedback to students and parents about performance and progress within a reasonable time frame.

c. The teacher uses acceptable grading/ranking/scoring practices in recording and reporting student achievements.

Performance Standard **A-3**   **The teacher uses assessment results to make both daily and long-range instructional decisions.**

Sample Performance Indicators:

a. The teacher uses results of a variety of assessments to monitor and modify instruction as needed.

b. The teacher organizes, maintains, and uses records of student progress to make effective instructional decisions.

c. The teacher creates and evaluates assessment materials to ensure consistency with current course content.

d. The teacher uses assessments that reflect course content.

e. The teacher initiates appropriate interventions to address student academic and or behavioral concerns.

Domain E: Learning Environment

Performance Standard **E-1**   **The teacher maximizes the use of instructional time to increase student learning.**

Sample Performance Indicators:

a. The teacher plans and demonstrates effective routines and procedures.

b. The teacher structures transitions in an efficient and constructive manner.

c. The teacher assists students in planning and organizing for assignments, long-range projects, and tests.

d. The teacher involves the student in learning.

Performance Standard **E-2**   **The teacher demonstrates and models respect toward students and others.**

Sample Performance Indicators:

a. The teacher models caring, fairness, humor, courtesy, respect, and active listening.

b. The teacher models concern for student emotional and physical well-being.

c. The teacher seeks and maintains positive interactions with students.

Performance Standard **E-3**   **The teacher organizes the classroom to ensure a safe academic and physical learning environment.**

Sample Performance Indicators:

a. The teacher creates a physical setting that promotes learning and minimizes disruption.

b. The teacher complies with local, state, and federal safety regulations.

c. The teacher organizes the classroom to facilitate the monitoring of students' work and to provide assistance.

d. The teacher manages emergency situations, as they occur, in the school setting.

e. The teacher creates a learning setting in which the student feels free to take risks.

Performance Standard **E-4**   **The teacher communicates clear expectations about behavior to students and parents.**

Sample Performance Indicators:

a. The teacher monitors student behavior and provides feedback in a constructive manner to students and parents.

b. The teacher redirects students who are off-task.

c. The teacher enforces classroom/school rules.

d. The teacher minimizes the effects of disruptive behavior.

Domain P: Professionalism

Performance Standard **P-1**   **The teacher demonstrates ethical and professional behavior.**

Sample Performance Indicators:

a. The teacher demonstrates adherence to ethical and professional standards.

b. The teacher selects appropriate channels for resolving concerns and problems while maintaining confidentiality.

c. The teacher maintains professional relations with colleagues and others in the school community.

d. The teacher provides for student confidentiality.

Performance Standard **P-2**   **The teacher applies strategies learned from professional development.**

Sample Performance Indicators:

a. The teacher participates in professional growth activities including conferences, workshops, course work and committees, or membership in professional organizations.

b. The teacher explores, disseminates, and applies knowledge and information about new or improved methods of instruction and related issues.

c. The teacher evaluates and identifies areas of personal strength(s) and weakness(es) and seeks improvement of skills and professional performance.

Performance Standard **P-3** **The teacher contributes to the overall school climate by supporting school goals.**

Sample Performance Indicators:

a. The teacher shares teaching insights and coordinates learning activities for students.

b. The teacher serves on school committees and supports school activities.

c. The teacher contributes to the development of the profession by serving as a mentor, peer coach, or supervisor of student teachers.

d. The teacher completes all class and school responsibilities in a timely and effective manner.

e. The teacher carries out duties in accordance with established policies, practices, and regulations.

Performance Standard **P-4** **The teacher initiates and maintains timely communication with parents/guardians and administrators concerning student progress or problems.**

Sample Performance Indicators:

a. The teacher responds promptly to parental concerns.

b. The teacher encourages parental involvement within the school.

c. The teacher provides information regarding school/community functions to parents/guardians.

d. The teacher works with community members in carrying out school and community sponsored functions.

Appendix B

PERFORMANCE ASSESSMENT RUBRIC

Description of Performance Assessment Rubric

An Assessment Rubric has been developed to articulate four levels of performance for each of the 18 identified teacher performance standards. The Assessment Rubric provides a specific description of what the four ratings entail for each standard. Evaluators will make judgments about functioning at the performance-standard level based on the information collected through multiple data sources. This scale can be used for the summative evaluation for both tenured and nontenured teachers. Thus, the Assessment Rubric guides evaluators in assessing how well a standard is performed and provides a framework for greater consistency across teachers and schools.

Note: The performance standard is the expectation for Satisfactory performance.

Domain I: Instructional Skills

	Exemplary	Satisfactory	Needs Improvement	Unsatisfactory
Organizing for Instruction				
I-1	The teacher seeks and exhibits high level of knowledge of subject(s) taught and continually updates curriculum.	**The teacher demonstrates current and accurate knowledge of subject matter covered in the curriculum.**	The teacher lacks comprehensive knowledge of subject(s) taught or does not stay current with curriculum.	The teacher lacks knowledge of subject(s) taught and does not stay current or follow the curriculum.
I-2	The teacher strives to improve planning so that appropriate curriculum objectives, learning activities, and lesson plans ensure active learning of all students.	**The teacher plans instruction to achieve desired student learning objectives that reflect current district curriculum.**	The teacher plans instruction that does not focus on student learning and/or does not follow the district curriculum objectives.	The teacher does not plan adequate lessons.
I-3	The teacher selects, creates, and uses a variety of materials and resources compatible with student needs/abilities that support the current district curriculum.	**The teacher uses materials and resources compatible with students' needs and abilities that support the current district curriculum.**	The teacher inconsistently uses materials and resources that are compatible with student needs/abilities or that support the current district curriculum.	The teacher uses materials and resources incompatible with student needs/abilities and/or that do not support the current district curriculum.

	Exemplary	Satisfactory	Needs Improvement	Unsatisfactory
I-4	The teacher uses a variety of strategies to link instruction with past and future student learning experiences, other subject areas, and real-world experiences/applications.	**The teacher links present content/skills with past and future learning experiences, other subject areas, and real-world experiences/applications.**	The teacher does not consistently link instruction with past and future learning experiences, other subject areas, or real-world experiences/applications.	The teacher does not link instruction with past and future learning experiences, other subject areas, or real-world experiences/applications.

Delivery of Instruction

	Exemplary	Satisfactory	Needs Improvement	Unsatisfactory
I-5	The teacher communicates effectively with individual students and classroom groups, uses standard English, and serves as an exemplary model for public speaking.	**The teacher communicates effectively with students and models standard English.**	The teacher does not consistently communicate effectively with students or does not model standard English.	The teacher does not communicate effectively with students and does not model standard English.
I-6	The teacher develops and uses a variety of instructional strategies to promote student learning.	**The teacher uses a variety of instructional strategies to promote student learning.**	The teacher uses a limited variety of instructional strategies.	The teacher does not use a variety of instructional strategies to promote student learning.

Domain A: Assessment Skills

	Exemplary	Satisfactory	Needs Improvement	Unsatisfactory
A-1	The teacher creates, selects, and effectively uses a variety of ongoing and culminating assessments.	**The teacher provides a variety of ongoing and culminating assessments to measure student performance.**	The teacher uses a limited variety of ongoing and culminating assessments.	The teacher does not use a variety of ongoing and culminating assessments.
A-2	The teacher uses, interprets, and effectively communicates assessment results to encourage student progress.	**The teacher provides ongoing feedback to encourage student progress.**	The teacher provides limited feedback to encourage student progress.	The teacher does not provide ongoing feedback to encourage student progress.
A-3	The teacher evaluates and uses a wide variety of assessment materials and strategies to make daily and long-range instructional decisions.	**The teacher uses assessment results to make daily and long-range instructional decisions.**	The teacher inconsistently uses assessment results to make daily and/or long-range instructional decisions.	The teacher does not use assessment results to make daily and long-range instructional decisions.

Domain E: Learning Environment

	Exemplary	Satisfactory	Needs Improvement	Unsatisfactory
E-1	The teacher uses exemplary organizational strategies to manage instructional time and increase student learning.	**The teacher maximizes the use of instructional time to increase student learning.**	The teacher does not consistently manage instructional time effectively to increase student learning.	The teacher uses instructional time poorly, resulting in lost opportunity for student learning.
E-2	The teacher consistently demonstrates and actively promotes respect toward students and others.	**The teacher demonstrates and models respect toward students and others.**	The teacher inconsistently demonstrates respect toward students or others.	The teacher demonstrates disrespect toward students or others.
E-3	The teacher consistently maintains a safe physical and positive academic learning environment that promotes active learning.	**The teacher organizes the classroom to ensure a safe academic and physical learning environment.**	The teacher maintains a safe physical environment but does not always provide a positive learning environment.	The teacher does not organize or maintain a safe physical or positive academic environment.
E-4	The teacher communicates clear expectations for behavior and helps students meet those expectations in a positive and constructive manner.	**The teacher communicates clear expectations about behavior to students and parents.**	The teacher inconsistently communicates expectations for behavior to students and parents.	The teacher does not communicate clear expectations for behavior to students and parents.

Domain P: Professionalism

	Exemplary	Satisfactory	Needs Improvement	Unsatisfactory
P-1	The teacher models ethical and professional behavior and consistently interacts with students, staff, and community in a positive manner.	**The teacher demonstrates ethical and professional behavior.**	The teacher inconsistently demonstrates ethical or professional behavior.	The teacher demonstrates unethical or unprofessional behavior.
P-2	The teacher participates in, seeks out, and shares professional development activities.	**The teacher applies strategies learned from professional development.**	The teacher makes limited use of strategies gained through professional development.	The teacher shows little or no interest in professional development.
P-3	The teacher contributes to a positive school climate by initiating and actively supporting school goals.	**The teacher contributes to the overall school climate by supporting school goals.**	The teacher inconsistently demonstrates support for school goals.	The teacher does not demonstrate support for school goals.
P-4	The teacher proactively consults, communicates, and works with parents/guardians and administrators concerning student progress or problems.	**The teacher initiates and maintains timely communication with parents/guardians and administrators concerning student progress or problems.**	The teacher inconsistently initiates and maintains timely communication with parents/guardians and administrators concerning student progress or problems.	The teacher does not initiate or maintain timely communication with parents/guardians and administrators concerning student progress or problems.

Appendix C

GENERAL GUIDELINES FOR ORGANIZING A TEACHER PORTFOLIO

Professional Teacher Portfolio

Suggestions:

- ◆ Decide on a standard size notebook for the portfolio.

- ◆ Order the notebooks in bulk and in specific colors as desired.

- ◆ Order the notebooks with specific covers designed for each school.

- ◆ Order notebooks with acetate covers front and back for top-loading school-specific identifier sheets.

Teacher Name: _____

School Name: _____

Contents from _____ to _____
                    (month/year)   (month/year)

Teacher Portfolio

Table of Contents

Yourtown Public Schools

Performance Standards and Assessment System

Guidelines for Teacher Portfolio

Yourtown Public Schools

Purpose

The teacher portfolio is an important component of a multiple data source evaluation system. The goals of the teacher portfolio are to enhance classroom instruction, advance professional growth, and document both student learning and teacher performance. The portfolio provides the teacher with an opportunity for self-reflection, demonstration of quality work, and a basis for two-way communication with an evaluator. In compiling the portfolio, emphasis should be placed on quality, not quantity, and evidence that clearly focuses on specific teacher responsibilities.

> **The purpose of the portfolio is to document teaching excellence. The portfolio provides the teacher with an opportunity for self-reflection, demonstration of quality work, and a basis for two-way communication with an evaluator. The emphasis is on the quality, *not* the quantity of materials presented.**

Procedures and Format

The teacher will compile a portfolio as part of each summative evaluation process. Portfolio documentation will be placed in a one-inch, three-ring binder with dividers supplied by Yourtown Schools. The teacher will compile and maintain documentation in each of four evaluation domains: Instructional Skills, Assessment Skills, Learning Environment Skills, and Professionalism.

The portfolio is to contain the following: Yourtown Schools' cover page, a resume, and documentation from each of the four skill domains. The divider page will list the responsibilities for that domain. The teacher will complete the contents page for each domain as a guide to the evaluator.

In constructing the portfolio, teachers should follow this outline:

- ◆ **Domain I: Instructional Skills**
  - A minimum of four performance standards must be addressed.
  - This section must include a lesson plan and resulting student work.
- ◆ **Domain A: Assessment Skills**
  - A minimum of two performance standards must be addressed.
  - One item should document student growth.
- ◆ **Domain E: Learning Environment Skills**
  - A minimum of two performance standards must be addressed.
  - A copy of your behavior management plan or class rules must be included.
- ◆ **Domain P: Professionalism**
  - A minimum of two performance standards must be addressed.
  - This section must contain a log of professional growth activities, such as the record of recertification points.

Your Portfolio...

- ◆ is a one-inch, three-ring binder with a cover and section dividers possibly provided by the school division.
- ◆ contains only the items you wish to present to your evaluator. *You have full responsibility for the contents, pacing, and development.*
- ◆ is limited to items that will fit within the binder. Larger items can be photographed or photocopied for inclusion. *Artifacts that do not fit in the binder (e.g., video or audio tapes) may be submitted separately.*
- ◆ remains in your possession except when reviewed by your evaluator. *(It should be available during evaluation conferences.)*
- ◆ belongs to you *(even if you change schools or leave the school division).*
- ◆ is one component of a multiple source evaluation system *(which also includes observations, customer focus data, student performance data, and other relevant information).*

Procedures...

- ◆ Insert the *Checklist* for each domain directly behind the proper divider and place your documentation in the corresponding section. (Note: This will be an ongoing process and the portfolio will not be complete until the end of the three-year evaluation cycle).
- ◆ Include as many activities as are needed to document the standards in each domain.

♦ File completed documentation behind the appropriate divider. If an item satisfies more than one standard, it can be referenced in other sections by a notation on the checklist.

Review...

♦ Your evaluator (principal, assistant principal, instructional coordinator, or other direct supervisor) will not grade your portfolio. Rather, the evaluator will review the portfolio as part of the overall assessment of your work quality.

♦ Your portfolio provides documentation that complements the observation component of the multiple data evaluation system.

♦ Your evaluator will look for evidence in the portfolio and through observation to determine that you meet the standards and expectations stated in the Yourtown Public Schools *Teacher Performance Standards and Assessment System Handbook.*

♦ Your evaluator and you will review and discuss the contents of the portfolio during periodic performance review conferences.

Hints...

♦ Work on your portfolio over time.

♦ Obtain a file folder to store potential items until you are ready to put them in the portfolio.

♦ Begin working on the *Assessment* and *Professionalism* sections first because the standards in these domains cannot be observed as readily as can standards in other domains.

♦ Make your portfolio user-friendly (i.e., neat, organized) so that your documentation is concise, clear, and easily located.

♦ Have your portfolio available every time you meet with your evaluator. Even though it is a "work in progress" and not complete until the end of your three-year evaluation cycle, use it to document your ongoing professional growth and development.

♦ Include brief reflective comments or explanations to accompany the activities you choose for documentation (as necessary).

♦ Place a current résumé in the front of your portfolio.

Sample Activities for Documenting Standards in Each Domain…

Instruction

- summary of a plan for integrating instruction or services or for creating interdisciplinary units (e.g., integrating language arts and science)

- written evidence of integrating writing and content reading into classroom instruction (e.g., a *list* of reading and writing activities in content lessons)

- annotated list of instructional activities for a unit

- outline of a lesson with differentiation for multiple ability levels and learning styles

- evidence of an enrichment activity (e.g., field trip, speaker, resource file)

- annotated photographs of teacher-made displays used in instruction

- annotated samples or photographs of instructional materials written/created by you

- lesson/intervention plan (including goals and objectives, activities, resources, and assessment measures)

- summary of consultation with appropriate staff members regarding special needs of individual students

- examples of student work

- audio/video tape of a lesson

- description of a strategy used to meet individual student needs

- sample of teacher made instructional materials

- complete unit plan with instructional objectives, activities, student work and assessments

- lesson plan or student work demonstrating technology integration

- list of resources and strategies used to update subject matter.

- content course work or workshops attended

- photographs/videos/student products demonstrating skills application

Assessment

- ♦ brief report describing your record-keeping system and how it is used to monitor student progress

- ♦ copy of teacher-made tests or other assessment measures (e.g., professional testing materials, informal assessment measures, student-generated assessment measures)

- ♦ copy of the scoring rubric used for a student project

- ♦ summary explaining grading procedures

- ♦ photocopies or photographs of student work with your written comments

- ♦ samples of educational reports, progress reports, or letters prepared for parents or students

- ♦ demonstration of an instructional decision based on assessment results

Learning Environment

- ♦ list of appropriate rules for the classroom with a brief explanation of the procedures used to develop them

- ♦ diagram of your classroom with identifying comments

- ♦ diagram of alternative classroom arrangements for special purposes, with explanatory comments

- ♦ schedule of daily classroom routines

- ♦ explanation of behavior management philosophy and procedures

- ♦ log of attempts to establish and maintain rapport through such measures as parent calls, personal notes, interventions, personal conferences, interest surveys, and extracurricular school activities

- ♦ description of how you have managed a disruptive student or situation

- ♦ video of student behavior in classroom setting

- ♦ communication to parents about expectations or actual student behavior

- ♦ examples of time management strategies

- ♦ safety rules and the means of documenting student understanding of them

Professionalism

- documentation of participation in professional societies and organizations

- evidence of achievement and recognition, such as letters of recommendation, receipt of grants, and information on any awards received

- evidence of supervision of pre-service education students, student teachers, or graduate student interns

- documentation of participation on committees, task forces, etc.

- annotated list of school activities you supervised (e.g., after-school or extracurricular activities)

- documentation of collateral professional duties such as mentoring, shadowing, or peer partnerships

- evidence of courses taught for a school district, college, university, or other educational institution, separate from annual contract responsibilities

- log of in-service/staff development activities

- annotated list of subject-related courses completed and/or seminars, workshops, or conferences attended

- post-graduate college transcript, accompanied by a brief explanation of the purpose for graduate study (e.g., further degree plans, pursue additional endorsements, recertification studies)

- annotated log documenting collaboration with teammates, other teachers and specialists, and other professional educators

- evidence of professional presentations in courses, workshops, conference sessions, etc. (e.g., a copy of the agenda or program, or a dated/annotated copy of handouts used, or a copy of a speech given, or photographs of the professional presentation)

- copy of any material submitted for publication in professional journals, newsletters, etc., (including a copy as published or a brief description of progress toward publication)

- a project or product produced with a colleague

- annotated log of parent or community contacts

Contents of Section

NOTE: The teacher should fill out this table of contents for each responsibility area of the portfolio and place it immediately behind the divider for that section to serve as a guide for the reviewer.

Item #___

Description of Item:

Responsibility Documented:

Context and Date Used:

Teacher Comment:

Item #___

Description of Item:

Responsibility Documented:

Context and Date Used:

Teacher Comment:

Appendix D

PERFORMANCE STANDARDS CROSS-REFERENCED WITH SAMPLE ARTIFACTS

Performance Standards	*Examples of Materials to Document Performance Standards*
I-1	1. A log of in-service/staff development activities for the evaluation period (ongoing activities could be listed one time, with the inclusive dates noted)
I-1	2. Post-graduate college transcript
I-2, I-6, I-7	3. Evidence of substitute teacher plan and/or plans for teacher assistants, student teachers
I-1, I-4, I-6, I-7, P-3	4. A written review of a new textbook with potential for adoption by the division
I-1, P-2	5. A list of subject-related courses completed and seminars, workshops, or conferences attended during the evaluation period
I-1, I-2, I-3, I-6	6. A report with suggestions for integrating instruction or creating interdisciplinary units as it applies to the teacher's assignment (such as integrating language arts and art)
I-3, I-6	7. Written evidence of integrating writing and content reading into classroom instruction
I-1, I-2, I-3, I-5	8. Representative course syllabi
I-1, I-2, I-3, I-4, I-5, I-6, I-7, A-3	9. A lesson plan with goals, objectives, activities, resources, and evaluation
I-2, I-3, I-6, I-7	10. A list of instructional activities for a unit
I-1, I-2, I-3, I-6, I-7	11. An outline of a lesson with differentiation for multiple ability levels and learning styles
I-2, I-3, I-6, I-7	12. Evidence of participation in planning for a field trip, speaker, or other enrichment activity (lists, logs, copies of documents)
I-1, I-2, I-4	13. Teacher's rationale for and examples of sequencing instructional topics

Performance Standards	Examples of Materials to Document Performance Standards
I-3, I-6, I-7	14. Evidence of multiple (three or more) techniques for solving a problem (such as in math) or presenting an issue (such as the use of nuclear energy to generate power, the use/abuse of the rain forests, a study of affirmative action, or how to critique a work of art) directly related to the teacher's current assignment
I-1, I-2, I-3	15. A list of those school and community sources of materials and human resources available to the teacher and verified for availability within the evaluation period
I-3, I-6, I-7	16. A log on the use of available technology by the teacher and students
I-1, I-3	17. Photographs with explanations of teacher-made displays used in instruction within the year
I-2, I-6, I-7	18. Samples or photographs of teacher-written instructional materials
Any	19. Other activity demonstrating instructional skill (to be designed by the teacher, reviewed with the evaluator, and specified here): As an example, the teacher could write a description of efforts taken to improve his/her own teaching
I-1, I-2, I-4, I-6, I-7, A-1, A-2	20. Copies of teacher-made tests or evidence of student assessment procedures (such as professional testing materials, informal assessment measures, student-generated assessment measures)
I-2, I-4, I-6, I-7, A-1, A-2	21. A copy of the scoring rubrics used for a student project or report
A-1, A-2, P-1	22. Explanation of grading procedures
I-4, A-1, A-2, P-1	23. A report describing the teacher's record-keeping system and how it is used to monitor student progress
I-1, I-2, I-3, I-4, I-5, I-6, I-7, A-1, P-1	24. Copies or photographs of graded student work with comments from the teacher written on them (may be photocopies, with students' names and other identifying information blanked out)

Performance Standards	*Examples of Materials to Document Performance Standards*
I-5, A-1, P-4	25. Samples of the progress reports/letters prepared for parents/guardians or given to students (if individualized, identifying information about students must be blanked out)
Any	26. Other activity demonstrating skill in assessment (to be designed by the teacher, reviewed by the evaluator, and specified here):
I-6, E-2, E-4	27. List of appropriate classroom rules with a written explanation of the procedures used to develop them
I-6, E-3, E-4	28. Diagram of classroom with identifying commentary
I-6, E-3, E-4	29. Diagram of alternative classroom arrangements for special purposes, with explanatory commentary
I-5, I-7, E-1, E-3	30. Log of daily classroom schedule/routine
I-5, I-7, E-1, E-3, P-2	31. Logs of routines as adapted for instructional or administrative reasons (such as half-days or assembly schedules)
E-3	32. Evidence of emergency and safety procedures briefing for students
E-3, E-4, P-1, P-4	33. Explanation of behavior management philosophy and procedures
I-7, E-2, E-4, P-1, P-3, P-4	34. Annotated log of attempts to establish and maintain rapport through such measures as teacher calls, personal notes, interventions, personal conferences, interest surveys, and advanced and extracurricular school activities
Any	35. Other activity demonstrating skill in management (to be designed by the teacher, reviewed by the evaluator, and specified here):
I-2, P-1, P-2, P-3, P-4	36. Statement of teaching responsibilities
I-1, I-2, I-3, I-4, I-6, I-7, P-3	37. A log documenting collaboration, including collaboration with teammates, other teachers, and other professional educators within and across disciplines

Performance Standards	Examples of Materials to Document Performance Standards
I-1, P-2	38. Evidence of professional presentations in courses, workshops, conference sessions, etc.
I-1, P-2	39. Copies of any materials submitted to professional newsletters and journals or other publications
I-1, P-2	40. Documentation of teacher participation in learned societies and professional organizations
I-1, P-2, P-4	41. Evidence of achievement and recognition, such as letters of recommendation, receipt of grants, and information on any awards received (e.g., certificate, letter, newspaper article)
I-1, P-2	42. Review of a professional book
I-1, P-2	43. Journal with brief reviews/abstracts of professional articles read
I-1, I-2, I-3, I-4, I-6, I-7, P-1, P-3	44. Summary of consultation with appropriate staff members (such as special education teachers, resource specialists, school psychologists, the school nurse) regarding special needs of individual students
I-2, P-3	45. Evidence of supervision of student teachers, education laboratory students, or clinical education students
P-3	46. Documentation of participation in committees on which teacher served during the evaluation period
P-3, P-4	47. A list of after-school activities that the teacher supervised during the evaluation period
P-3, P-4	48. A list of collateral responsibilities assumed during the evaluation period (e.g., supervising the student bookstore before school, writing school publicity, organizing parent volunteers, serving as social committee chair)
I-3, P-3, P-4	49. Documentation of collaboration with other professionals (i.e., mentoring, shadowing, peer partnerships)

Performance Standards	*Examples of Materials to Document Performance Standards*
P-3, P-4	50. A collection of parent/guardian and/or school/community communications and activities, including examples such as newsletters, committee meetings or functions, PTA meetings, and partnership involvement
I-1, I-2, I-3, I-4, I-5, I-6, I-7, P-2	51. Evidence of individual exploration/study/project/commitment in an endeavor directly related to instructional competence
I-1, I-2, I-3, I-4, I-5, I-6, I-7, P-2	52. Evidence of individual exploration/study/project/commitment in an endeavor directly related to knowledge of subject matter
A-1, A-2, A-3, P-2	53. Evidence of individual exploration/study/project/commitment in an endeavor directly related to assessment competence
E-1, E-2, E-3, E-4, P-2	54. Evidence of individual exploration/study/project/commitment in an endeavor directly related to competency in classroom management
P-1, P-2, P-3, P-4	55. Evidence of individual exploration/study/project/commitment in an endeavor directly related to demonstration of professionalism
P-1, P-2, P-3, P-4	56. Evidence of individual exploration/study/project/commitment in an endeavor directly related to performance of other duties at school or in the community
Any	57. Other activity demonstrating professionalism (to be designed by the teacher, reviewed by the evaluator, and specified here): for instance, the teacher might include previous written evaluations or copies of written evaluations, with or without accompanying commentary

Appendix E

SAMPLE ARTIFACTS CROSS-REFERENCED WITH PERFORMANCE STANDARDS

Domain I—Instructional Skills

(Numbered examples of materials are keyed to master list in Appendix D.)

Examples of Materials to Document Performance Standards	*I-1*	*I-2*	*I-3*	*I-4*	*I-5*	*I-6*	*I-7*
1. Log of in-service/staff development activities	X						
2. Post-graduate college transcript	X						
3. Plans for substitutes/teacher assistants		X				X	X
4. Written review of a new textbook	X			X		X	X
5. Subject-related courses/seminars/lectures	X						
6. Plan for integrating/interdisciplinary units	X	X	X			X	
7. Integrate writing with content reading			X			X	
8. Representative course syllabi	X	X	X		X		
9. Lesson plan with goals, objectives, evaluation	X	X	X	X	X	X	X
10. List of instructional activities for a unit		X	X			X	X
11. Differentiated lesson outline	X	X	X			X	X
12. Plan a field trip/speaker/enrichment activity		X	X			X	X
13. Rationale/examples of sequenced instruction	X	X		X			
14. Present multiple techniques to problem solve			X			X	X
15. List community and available human resources	X	X	X				
16. Log use of technology			X			X	X
17. Photo with explanations of teacher-made displays	X		X				
18. Samples of teacher-written instructional materials		X				X	X
19. Other activity demonstrating instructional skill	X	X	X	X	X	X	X

Examples of Materials to Document Performance Standards	I-1	I-2	I-3	I-4	I-5	I-6	I-7
20. Copies of teacher-made tests/assessment materials	X	X		X		X	X
21. Scoring rubrics used for student project or report		X		X		X	X
23. Report describing teacher's record keeping system				X			
24. Copies of student work with teachers comments	X	X	X	X	X	X	X
25. Sample progress reports/letters for parents					X		
26. Other activity demonstrating skill in assessment	X	X	X	X	X	X	X
27. Classroom rules with procedures used to develop them						X	
28. Diagram of classroom with identifying commentary						X	
29. Diagram of alternate/special use class arrangement						X	
30. Log of daily classroom schedule/routine					X		X
31. Logs of class schedule for non-standard day					X		X
34. Log of attempts to establish rapport with parents							X
35. Other activity demonstrating skill in management	X	X	X	X	X	X	X
36. Statement of teaching responsibilities		X					
37. Document collaboration within and across disciplines	X	X	X	X		X	X
38. Professional conference/workshop presentations	X						
39. Material submitted for professional publication	X						
40. Document participation in professional organizations	X						
41. Evidence of achievement/recognition/awards/grants	X						
42. Review of a professional book	X						

Examples of Materials to Document Performance Standards	*I-1*	*I-2*	*I-3*	*I-4*	*I-5*	*I-6*	*I-7*
43. Journal with reviews/abstracts of professional articles	X						
44. Summary of consultations for special needs students	X	X	X	X		X	X
45. Evidence of supervision of student teachers/interns		X					
49. Document collaboration with other professionals			X				
51. Instructional competency-related exploration/project X	X	X	X	X	X	X	X
52. Subject matter knowledge-related project	X	X	X	X	X	X	X
57. Other activity demonstrating professionalism	X	X	X	X	X	X	X

Domain A—Assessment Skills

(Numbered examples of materials are keyed to master list in Appendix D.)

Examples of Materials to Document Performance Standards	A-1	A-2	A-3
9. Lesson plan with goals, objectives, evaluation		X	
19. Other activity demonstrating instructional skill	X	X	X
20. Copies of teacher-made tests/assessment materials	X	X	
21. Scoring rubrics used for student project or report	X	X	
22. Explanation of grading procedures	X	X	
23. Report describing teacher's record keeping system	X	X	
24. Copies of student work with teachers comments	X		
25. Sample progress reports/letters for parents	X		
26. Other activity demonstrating skill in assessment	X	X	X
35. Other activity demonstrating skill in management	X	X	X
53. Assessment-related exploration/project	X	X	
57. Other activity demonstrating professionalism	X	X	X

Domain E—Learning Environment

(Numbered examples of materials are keyed to master list in Appendix D.)

Examples of Materials to Document Performance Standards	E-1	E-2	E-3	E-4
19. Other activity demonstrating instructional skill	X	X	X	X
26. Other activity demonstrating skill in assessment	X	X	X	X
27. Classroom rules with procedures used to develop them		X		X
28. Diagram of classroom with identifying commentary			X	X
29. Diagram of alternate/special use class arrangement			X	X
30. Log of daily classroom schedule/routine	X		X	
31. Logs of class schedule for nonstandard day	X		X	
32. Evidence of emergency/safety briefings to students			X	
33. Explanation of behavior management philosophy			X	X
34. Log of attempts to establish rapport with parents		X		X
35. Other activity demonstrating skill in management	X	X	X	X
54. Classroom management-related exploration/project	X	X	X	X
57. Other activity demonstrating professionalism	X	X	X	X

Domain P—Professionalism

(Numbered examples of materials are keyed to master list in Appendix D.)

Examples of Materials to Document Performance Standards	*P-1*	*P-2*	*P-3*	*P-4*
4. Written review of a new textbook			X	
5. Subject-related courses/seminars/lectures		X		
19. Other activity demonstrating instructional skill	X	X	X	X
22. Explanation of grading procedures	X			
23. Report describing teacher's record keeping system	X			
24. Copies of student work with teachers comments	X			
25. Sample progress reports/letters for parents				X
26. Other activity demonstrating skill in assessment	X	X	X	X
30. Log of daily classroom schedule/routine	X	X		
31. Logs of class schedule for nonstandard day		X		
33. Explanation of behavior management philosophy	X			X
34. Log of attempts to establish rapport with parents	X		X	X
35. Other activity demonstrating skill in management	X	X	X	X
36. Statement of teaching responsibilities	X	X	X	X
37. Document collaboration within and across disciplines			X	
38. Professional conference/workshop presentations		X		
39. Material submitted for professional publication		X		
40. Document participation in professional organizations		X		
41. Evidence of achievement/recognition/awards/ grants		X		X
42. Review of a professional book		X		
43. Journal with reviews/abstracts of professional articles		X		

Examples of Materials to Document Performance Standards	P-1	P-2	P-3	P-4
44. Summary of consultations for special needs students	X		X	
45. Evidence of supervision of student teachers/interns			X	
46. Document participation on committees			X	
47. List of teacher-supervised after-school activities			X	X
48. List of collateral responsibilities			X	X
49. Document collaboration with other professionals			X	X
50. Collection of parent/school/community newsletters			X	X
51. Instructional competency-related exploration/project		X		
52. Subject matter knowledge-related project		X		
54. Classroom management-related exploration/project		X		
55. Professionalism-related exploration/project	X	X	X	X
56. School/community duties-related exploration/project	X	X	X	X
57. Other activity demonstrating professionalism	X	X	X	X

Appendix F

PORTFOLIO FEEDBACK FORM

Yourtown Public Schools
Teacher Portfolio Feedback Form

_____	_____
Teacher	*Date*
_____	_____
Supervisor	*Time*

Part 1: Portfolio Review

Directions: Please read the following statements carefully and then respond to the statements by checking (✔) the most appropriate descriptor based on your review of the teacher's portfolio. Definitions for each of the terms are given at the end of the form. If the statement does not apply to the teacher, check "NA." Please provide evidence for each teaching standard. Numbered "Applicable Activities" are keyed to master list in Appendix D.

Instructional Skills: Organizing for Instruction

	Clear Evidence	*Some Evidence*	*Little or No Evidence*	*NA*
I-1. The teacher demonstrates current and accurate knowledge of subject matter covered in the curriculum. **Applicable Activities:** 1, 2, 4, 5, 6, 8, 9, 11, 13, 15, 17, 19, 20, 24, 26, 35, 37, 38, 39, 40, 41, 42, 43, 44, 51, 52, 57				

EVIDENCE:

I-2. The teacher plans instruction to achieve desired student learning objectives that reflect current district curriculum. **Applicable Activities:** 3, 6, 8, 9, 10, 11, 12, 13, 15, 18, 19, 20, 21, 24, 26, 35, 36, 37, 55, 56, 51, 52, 57	*Clear Evidence*	*Some Evidence*	*Little or No Evidence*	*NA*

EVIDENCE:

I-3. The teacher uses materials and resources compatible with students' needs and abilities that support the current division curriculum. **Applicable Activities:** 6, 7, 8, 9, 10, 11, 12, 14, 15, 16, 17, 19, 24, 26, 35, 37, 44, 49, 51, 52, 57	*Clear Evidence*	*Some Evidence*	*Little or No Evidence*	*NA*

EVIDENCE:

I-4. The teacher links present content/skills with past and future learning experiences, other subject areas, and real world experiences/applications. **Applicable Activities:** 4, 9, 13, 19, 20, 21, 23, 24, 26, 35, 37, 44, 51, 52, 57	*Clear Evidence*	*Some Evidence*	*Little or No Evidence*	*NA*

EVIDENCE:

Instructional Skills: Delivery of Instruction

I-5. The teacher communicates effectively with students and models standard English. **Applicable Activities:** 8, 9, 19, 24, 25, 26, 30, 31, 35, 51, 52, 57	*Clear Evidence*	*Some Evidence*	*Little or No Evidence*	*NA*

EVIDENCE:

I-6. The teacher uses a variety of instructional strategies that promote student learning. **Applicable Activities:** 3, 4, 6, 7, 9, 10, 11, 12, 14, 16, 18, 19, 20, 21, 24, 26, 27, 28, 29, 35, 37, 44, 51, 52, 57	*Clear Evidence*	*Some Evidence*	*Little or No Evidence*	*NA*

EVIDENCE:

I-7. The teacher provides learning opportunities for individual differences. **Applicable Activities:** 3, 4, 9, 10, 11, 12, 14, 16, 18, 19, 20, 21, 24, 26, 30, 31, 34, 35, 37, 44, 51, 52, 57	*Clear Evidence*	*Some Evidence*	*Little or No Evidence*	*NA*

EVIDENCE:

Assessment Skills

A-1. The teacher provides a variety of on-going and culminating assessments to measure student performance. **Applicable Activities:** 19, 20, 21, 22, 23, 24, 25, 26, 35, 53, 57	*Clear Evidence*	*Some Evidence*	*Little or No Evidence*	*NA*

EVIDENCE:

A-2. The teacher provides ongoing and timely feedback to encourage student progress. **Applicable Activities:** 19, 20, 21, 22, 23, 26, 35, 53, 57	*Clear Evidence*	*Some Evidence*	*Little or No Evidence*	*NA*

EVIDENCE:

A-3. The teacher uses assessments to make both daily and long-range instructional decisions. **Applicable Activities:** 9, 19, 26, 35, 53, 57	*Clear Evidence*	*Some Evidence*	*Little or No Evidence*	*NA*

EVIDENCE:

Management Skills

Note: Management skills are not included on this form because they are performance standards that likely would not be represented in the Teacher Portfolio.

Professionalism

P-1. The teacher demonstrates ethical and professional behavior. **Applicable Activities:** 19, 22, 23, 24, 26, 33, 34, 35, 36, 44, 55, 56, 57	*Clear Evidence*	*Some Evidence*	*Little or No Evidence*	*NA*

EVIDENCE:

P-2. The teacher participates in an ongoing process of professional development. **Applicable Activities:** 5, 19, 26, 31, 35, 36, 38, 39, 40, 41, 42, 43, 51,42, 54, 55, 56, 57	*Clear Evidence*	*Some Evidence*	*Little or No Evidence*	*NA*

EVIDENCE:

P-3. The teacher contributes to the overall school climate by supporting school goals. **Applicable Activities:** 4, 19, 26, 34, 35, 36, 37, 44, 45, 46, 47, 48, 49, 50, 55, 56, 57	*Clear Evidence*	*Some Evidence*	*Little or No Evidence*	*NA*

EVIDENCE:

P-4. The teacher initiates and maintains timely communication with parents/guardians and administrators concerning student progress or problems. **Applicable Activities:** 19, 25, 26, 33, 34, 35, 36, 41, 47, 48, 49, 50, 55, 56, 57	*Clear Evidence*	*Some Evidence*	*Little or No Evidence*	*NA*

EVIDENCE:

Part 2: Summary Comments

Based on the activities noted on this form, the following comments are provided:

Commendations:

Recommendations:

Appendix G

CLIENT SURVEYS

Description of Client Surveys

Client surveys represent an additional source of information on teacher performance. Client surveys are unique in that, although they are required for each teacher, the teacher will retain exclusive access to the results of the surveys regarding his or her performance. The sole purpose of client surveys is to provide feedback directly to the teacher for professional growth and development.

Students will be asked for feedback on specified areas of performance standards about which they are best qualified to respond. There are three different versions of the student survey to reflect developmental differences in students' ability to provide useful feedback to their teacher: K–3, 4–5, and 6–12. All surveys will be completed anonymously to promote honest feedback.

Teachers are expected to administer student surveys according to school district guidelines. Elementary classroom teachers administer student surveys to their home-base students during a specified year. Elementary resource teachers administer student surveys to one class at grade levels K, 2, and 4 during a specified year. Teachers at the middle and high school level should administer surveys to two student classes representative of their teaching assignment during a specified year. Surveys should be administered approximately mid-year. The teacher retains sole access to the student surveys. However, the teacher is encouraged to include a summary of the surveys in the portfolio.

Client Survey Summary

Grade _____

Subject _____(Please use a separate form for each subject.)

_____Elementary _____Middle _____High

Client Survey Summary

- ◆ Who is your survey population (i.e., who do you want to respond to your questionnaire)?

    _____Parents _____Students _____Other

- ◆ How did you distribute your questionnaires?

    _____U.S. Mail   _____Distributed directly to students
    _____Other

- ◆ How did you collect your questionnaires?

    _____U.S. Mail   _____Collected directly from students
    _____Other

- ◆ How many questionnaires did you distribute?

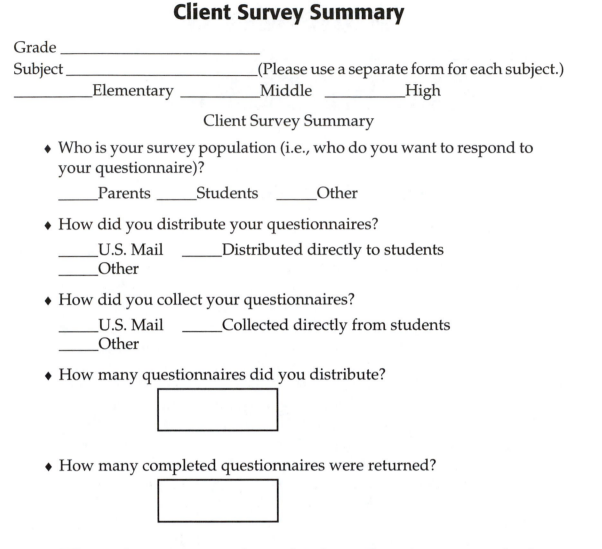

- ◆ How many completed questionnaires were returned?

- ◆ What is the percentage of completed questionnaires you received (#4 divided into #5)?

    %

Insert a copy of your questionnaire after this page.

Client Survey Analysis

♦ Describe your survey population(s) (i.e., list appropriate demographic characteristics such as grade level and subject for students).

♦ List factors that might have influenced the results (e.g., survey was conducted near time of report cards or progress reports).

♦ Analyze survey responses and answer the following questions:

What conclusions can you draw from the data?

a. What did the respondents perceive as your major strengths? (List 2 to 5 key strengths.)

b. Did respondents provide information that will help you select goals for continuous improvement? (List 1 to 2 potential goal areas suggested by the survey data.)

Suggestions for Interpreting Survey Data

♦ The purpose of a client survey is to collect information that will help you set goals for continuous improvement (i.e., for formative evaluation).

♦ Your clients are the individuals who use your services (e.g., students, parents, administrators, peers, coworkers). It is up to you to select the client group that can supply the most useful information for your personal and professional improvement.

♦ Remember, you are asking for your clients' perceptions. You are the only one who knows whether those perceptions provide an accurate measure of the quality of your service. However, if the respondents answer the questions honestly, the perceptions do provide a valid measure of satisfaction and should be worth knowing and considering.

♦ Look for trends in the data rather than responses from only one or two participants. It is extremely rare for 100 percent agreement in client perceptions. Focus on the majority of opinions.

♦ If 20 percent (or more) of your respondents provide the same general message, ask yourself the following questions:

  • Is the information your clients provided about you accurate?

  • If you agree that the information is accurate, are you satisfied with your clients' perceptions about you?

  • If you believe the information is inaccurate, do you know why your clients have these perceptions?

  • Do you need to make changes to improve your client's perceptions?

♦ If you think changes are justified, consider using the client data to set a personal or instructional goal for improvement.

Client Survey—Grades K–3

Yourtown Schools

Teacher Evaluation System   Student Survey

Directions: The teacher should read the following statements carefully to
students, and then request that the children respond to the statements by circling the face which shows whether they agree with
that sentence. The face with a smile means "yes," the face with a
straight mouth means "sometimes," and the face with an upside
down mouth means "no."

Teacher   *School Year*

		Yes	Sometimes	No
	Example: Chocolate is my favorite ice cream.	☺	😐	☹
1.	My teacher listens to me.	☺	😐	☹
2.	My teacher gives me help when I need it.	☺	😐	☹
3.	My teacher shows us how to do new things.	☺	😐	☹
4.	I know what I am supposed to do in class.	☺	😐	☹
5.	I am able to do the work in class.	☺	😐	☹
6.	I learn new things in my class.	☺	😐	☹

COMMENTS:

Client Survey–Grades 4–5

Yourtown Schools

Teacher Evaluation System   Student Survey

Directions: The teacher should read the following statements carefully to the students, and then request that the children respond to the statements by placing a check mark (✔) beneath the response—"YES," "SOMETIMES," or "NO"—that best describes whether they agree with that statement.

_____   _____
Teacher   *School Year*

		Yes	Sometimes	No
EXAMPLE:	I like listening to music.			
1.	My teacher listens to me.			
2.	My teacher gives me help when I need it.			
3.	My teacher shows us how to do new things.			
4.	I know what I am supposed to do in class.			
5.	I am able to do the work in class.			
6.	I learn new things in my class.			
7.	I feel safe in this class.			
8.	My teacher uses many ways to teach.			
9.	My teacher explains how my learning can be used outside school.			
10.	My teacher manages the class with few disruptions.			
11.	My teacher makes sure class time is used for teaching and learning.			
12.	My teacher explains why I get things wrong on my work.			
13.	My teacher shows respect to all students.			
14.	My teacher enforces disciplinary rules fairly and consistently.			

COMMENTS:

Client Survey—Grades 6–12

Yourtown Schools

Teacher Evaluation System   Student Survey

The purpose of this survey is to allow you to give your teacher ideas about how this class might be improved.

Directions: DO NOT PUT YOUR NAME ON THIS SURVEY. Write your class period in the space provided. Listed below are several statements about this class. Circle your response to each statement in the center column. If you wish to comment, please write your comments in the space after the item.

Teacher's Name	*School Year*	*Class Period*

In this class, my teacher...	*Circle One*	*Comments/ Examples*
1. gives clear instructions.	Yes Sometimes No	
2. treats everyone fairly.	Yes Sometimes No	
3. is available for help outside of class time.	Yes Sometimes No	
4. clearly states the objectives for the lesson.	Yes Sometimes No	
5. grades and returns my work in a reasonable time.	Yes Sometimes No	
6. relates lesson to other subjects or the real world.	Yes Sometimes No	

(turn over)

In this class, my teacher...	*Circle One*	*Comments/ Examples*
7. allows for and respects different opinions.	Yes Sometimes No	
8. encourages all students to learn.	Yes Sometimes No	
9. uses a variety of activities in class.	Yes Sometimes No	
10. communicates in a way I can understand.	Yes Sometimes No	
11. manages the classroom with a minimum of disruptions.	Yes Sometimes No	
12. shows respect to all students.	Yes Sometimes No	
13. enforces disciplinary rules fairly and consistently.	Yes Sometimes No	
14. makes sure class time is used for teaching and learning.	Yes Sometimes No	

COMMENTS:

Appendix H

PUBLIC DISSEMINATION PLAN

Yourtown Public Schools

Teacher Evaluation Committee
Teacher, Community, and Parent Involvement
Public Dissemination Plan

What are the purposes for involving others?
- ◆ to solicit feedback on concepts
- ◆ to solicit feedback on draft materials (i.e., edit)
- ◆ to inform
  - • throughout the development process
  - • at the end of the process
- ◆ to solicit support (i.e., ownership by teachers)

What are the possible strategies for involving others?
Teachers and Administrators:
- ◆ place monthly updates in school newsletters
- ◆ create *Fact Sheets*
  - • develop *Fact Sheets*
  - • distribute *Fact Sheets* in schools
- ◆ present information on progress at:
  - • faculty meetings at schools
  - • administrative meetings

Parents and Community
- ◆ invite school board members and PTA Council President to Evaluation Committee meetings or meet with them individually
- ◆ present and distribute *Fact Sheets* at PTA board meetings
- ◆ report at school board meetings

What should we disseminate?
   If there is a consensus that information about the development process and the specific elements of the proposed teacher evaluation system should be disseminated, then it will be important to determine *what* will be disseminated. *Fact Sheets* listed below could be a means of providing consistent information to convey to all parties.
- ◆ *Fact Sheet #1*—Overview of teacher evaluation system
- ◆ *Fact Sheet #2*—Teacher's performance standards
- ◆ *Fact Sheet #3*—Multiple data sources

Teacher Evaluation Committee
Teacher, Community, and Parent Involvement
Public Dissemination Timeline

Complete By	Activity	Responsible Party
	♦ develop *Fact Sheet #1*	
	♦ develop *Fact Sheet #2*	
	♦ write introduction to the development process for the new teacher evaluation system in the school newsletter	
	♦ distribute *Fact Sheet #1*	
	♦ provide update at School Board meeting	
	♦ provide update at Administrative Team meetings	
	♦ develop *Fact Sheet #3*	
	♦ include reminder on the new teacher evaluation system in the school newsletter	
	♦ hold meetings to discuss committee's work on teacher evaluation with interested faculty at each school	
	♦ distribute *Fact Sheet #2*	
	♦ circulate drafts of completed work (e.g., teacher responsibilities list)	
	♦ distribute *Fact Sheet #3*	
	♦ present overview of committee's work on teacher evaluation to PTA Council	
	♦ make presentation to School Board meeting	
	♦ provide update at administrative meeting	

Teacher Evaluation Committee

Teacher, Community, and Parent Involvement
Public Dissemination Timeline

Complete By	Activity	Responsible Party

Appendix I

SAMPLE NEWSLETTERS INTRODUCING THE CONCEPT OF PORTFOLIOS

Yourtown Public Schools' New Teacher Evaluation System

Fact Sheet #1: Overview	Spring 200X

TEACHER EVALUATION

Introduction

The current YPS teacher evaluation system has been in use since 1995. While it has served us well during the last several years, the direction of our schools has changed, and research now offers more guidance on how to make better use of evaluation for school improvement and professional growth. We are moving toward an evaluation system that is based on a more broadly-based approach to instruction. Additionally, the new evaluation system must take into consideration requirements passed by the 1999 State General Assembly requiring teacher evaluation be based on student safety, discipline, job responsibilities, and measures of student progress. Thus, it is time to re-examine our teacher evaluation system in light of these factors.

Purpose

One of the first questions the evaluation committee tackled was: What do we want from an evaluation system? We reviewed several possibilities in reaching consensus on the following issues:

- A new evaluation system should use a combination of effective teaching behaviors as well as general duties and responsibilities.
- The evaluation system should differentiate among different groups of teachers.
- The evaluation system should be based on multiple sources of information.
- The evaluation system should focus on high expectations for all employees.

In summary, what we hope to gain from a revamped evaluation system is twofold: 1) more accountability in teacher evaluation and 2) better support for professional development and school improvement.

How is the new evaluation system being developed?

The Board of Education charged the YPS Performance Management Committee with the responsibility to develop a new evaluation system that reflects current research and best practice in the area of personnel evaluation. Initial work of the committee involved discussion of basic philosophical and practical questions that provided a foundation and general direction. Once general agreement was reached on fundamental issues, the committee began the process of developing more specific elements of the new system, including procedures, guidelines, and materials. Draft copies of the work by the committee will be shared with teachers in each of the schools for their review and input.

Results of Strengths & Weaknesses Analysis

Before embarking upon a review of the research related to teacher evaluation and practices in other school systems across the country, we conducted a thorough review of our current evaluation system to determine what aspects of the system are valuable and should be preserved and which features need to be changed. The following is a summary of perceived strengths and weaknesses:

Strengths
- Written, positive, and immediate feedback
- Teacher/principal conferences
- Ease of administration
- Emphasis on classroom instructional techniques

Weaknesses
- Training in use of evaluation system not current
- Concern for reliability in rating performance
- Not comprehensive in nature

2   **YPS Performance Evaluation Fact Sheet**

- Lack of challenge for experienced teachers to grow professionally
- Not reflective of current teaching methods
- Evaluation based primarily on formal observation
- Job responsibilities of non-classroom teachers not addressed
- Lack of connection between teacher performance and student achievement
- System does not adequately distinguish among levels of performance

Who will be evaluated using the new evaluation system?

The evaluation system will be designed for use with all professional staff who are on the teacher salary schedule. We will develop evaluation guidelines first for classroom teachers. Once that is done, we will complete the development of the system for educational specialist positions (i.e., counselors, library-media specialists, speech pathologists). Additionally, there are plans to develop new evaluation guidelines for administrators in the fall, 20XX.

What are some of the new features being included?

- A format for evaluation that is flexible enough to be customized for all of the positions that will be included in the teacher evaluation system (i.e., classroom teacher, resource teacher, counselor)
- The development of more clearly defined roles and responsibilities for all teaching positions with evaluation of performance based on those defined roles
- The use of multiple sources of information about performance rather than just formal classroom observation
- A four point rating scale which emphasizes high quality performance

When will the new evaluation system be implemented?

Our goal is to have the new evaluation system completed for both classroom teachers and educational specialists by this summer. We anticipate implementing the new system in three schools on a pilot basis during the 200X-0X school year. Orientation and training will be provided for all administrators, teachers, and educational specialists included in the pilot.

How can I learn more about the teacher evaluation system?

There will be additional fact sheets addressing key aspects of the new teacher evaluation system. If you have questions or comments about the development process or other issues related to the teacher evaluation system, please talk with any of the following Performance Management Committee members:

Lois Alston	Harriet Greene	Pam Powell
Keisha Burns	Connie Jansen	Margee Ross
Francis Donovan	Cheryl Lantz	Maxine Simmons
Marshall Fitzgerald	Tracy Long	Valerie Wade
Jay Giles	Debbie Myers	

****

Yourtown Public Schools Performance Evaluation Committee: Teachers' Performance Standards

Fact Sheet # 2	Spring 200X

TEACHER PERFORMANCE EVALUATION

Introduction

The foundation of the new YPS teacher evaluation system is the use of clearly described and well-documented performance standards for all educators. In order for an evaluation system to be fair and comprehensive, it is necessary to describe the standards of teachers and other professionals with sufficient detail and accuracy so that both educators and their supervisors can reasonably understand the job expectations.

What are the teachers' performance standards?

A detailed description of the performance standards upon which the YPS teacher evaluation system will be based includes the following 18 performance domains:

Performance Domain: Instruction

I-1: The teacher demonstrates current and accurate knowledge of subject matter covered in the curriculum.

I-2: The teacher plans instruction to achieve desired student learning objectives that reflect current district curriculum standards.

I-3: The teacher uses materials and resources that are compatible with students' needs and abilities that support the district curriculum.

I-4: The teacher links present content/skills with past and future learning experiences, other subject areas, and real world experiences/applications.

I-5: The teacher communicates effectively with students and models standard English.

I-6 The teacher uses a variety of instructional strategies to promote student learning.

I-7 The teacher provides learning opportunities for individual differences.

Performance Domain: Assessment

A-1: The teacher uses a variety of ongoing and culminating assessments to measure student progress.

A-2: The teacher provides on-going and timely feedback to encourage student progress.

A-3: The teacher uses assessment results to make both daily and long-range instructional decisions.

Performance Domain: Learning Environment

E-1: The teacher maximizes the use of instructional time to increase student learning.

2   YPS Evaluation Fact Sheet: Teachers' Performance Standards

E-2:   The teacher demonstrates and models respect towards students and others.

E-3:   The teacher maintains a safe physical and positive academic learning environment.

E-4   The teacher communicates clear expectations about behavior to students and parents.

Performance Domain: Professionalism

P-1:   The teacher demonstrates ethical and professional behavior.

P-2:   The teacher applies strategies learned from professional development.

P-3:   The teacher contributes to the overall school climate by supporting school goals.

P-4   The teacher initiates and maintains timely communication with parents/ guardians and administrators concerning student progress or problems.

Summary

The complexity of the professional roles of teachers and other educators has increased significantly in the last two decades. Moreover, the standards-based performance expectations that exist in our state require an evaluation system that accounts for growth in student learning. If teachers and other educators are to be evaluated fully and fairly, an evaluation system must account for the complexities of their roles and responsibilities. It is the intent of the new YPS evaluation system to achieve this goal.

How can I learn more about the teacher evaluation system?

If you have questions or comments about the development process or other issues related to the teacher evaluation system, please talk with any of the Performance Management Committee members:

Lois Alston	Harriet Greene	Pam Powell
Keisha Burns	Connie Jansen	Margee Ross
Francis Donovan	Cheryl Lantz	Maxine Simmons
Marshall Fitzgerald	Tracy Long	Valerie Wade
Jay Giles	Debbie Myers	

YPS Evaluation Committee
Multiple Data Sources

Fact Sheet # 3   **Spring 200X**

TEACHER EVALUATION

Introduction

Teacher evaluation historically has relied heavily on classroom observations. This approach to evaluation has been formalized and developed as the clinical supervision model, in which the supervisor meets with the teacher during a pre-observation conference, observes the teacher, and then conducts a post-observation conference. In this teacher evaluation model, observation is often considered to be synonymous with evaluation.

Direct observation may be a useful way to collect information on teacher performance, but it does have major limitations. Among those limitations are the artificial nature of scheduled observations (when a special lesson is prepared for a special classroom visit) and the limited focus of the observation. If the purpose of a teacher evaluation system is to provide a comprehensive picture of performance in order to guide professional growth, then classroom observations should be only one piece of the information collected.

What sources will be included in the new teacher evaluation system?

The following information sources will be included in the new evaluation system to help document more comprehensively the performance of teachers and other professional employees.

Observation: While classroom observations do not serve well as the sole source for documenting performance, we do want observations to be part of a comprehensive data collection process. In addition to formal classroom observation, the new system will include *informal* observations (i.e., brief classroom visits) as a way to provide a fuller and fairer picture of performance. Both formal and informal observations will be focused on the educator's professional responsibilities.

Portfolios. A portion of the data collected to provide insight into a teacher's performance can be collected by the teacher. This does not necessarily require significant additional record-keeping. Some examples of records

include logs of meetings, lesson plans, samples of student work, teacher-developed materials, summaries of special activities completed, and copies of letters sent to or received from parents. This information can be organized as a portfolio of the teacher's performance in much the same way that a student's portfolio is organized.

Student academic goal setting. It is important that student academic progress be included as one factor in teacher evaluation. One method to implement this requirement is academic goal setting in which teachers document student academic benchmarks at the beginning of the school year, develop strategies to build on student strengths and address weaknesses, and document learning gains at the end of the year. Moreover, this approach is a research-based instructional strategy that can yield impressive gains in student learning.

How would multiple data sources be used in an evaluation?

It is important to remember that collecting feedback regarding personnel performance is not synonymous with evaluation. In an evaluation system that relies on multiple data sources, evidence of performance would be collected from a variety of sources, but it would be the supervisor who actually evaluates. In this type of system, however, the supervisor bases the evaluation on an analysis of the total evaluation portrait. Observation is only one source of information used in the evaluation.

If the supervisor and teacher have carefully designed ways to obtain feedback on specific job duties, there should be ample information to help make a well-founded and objective evaluation. For example, information about a teacher's instructional effectiveness may be obtained through formal and informal observations, a review of a portfolio, and student learning gains documented through academic goal setting. This more comprehensive approach to evaluation should provide a strong foundation upon which to develop improvement plans for the teacher and the school.

2   **YPS Evaluation Fact Sheet: Multiple Data Sources**

Summary

The complexity of professional roles in today's schools requires a performance evaluation that reflects that complexity. Multiple data sources enable the supervisor to obtain a more accurate picture of performance and assist the teacher in increasing student success.

How can I learn more about the teacher evaluation system?

If you have questions or comments about the development process or other issues related to the teacher evaluation system, please talk with any of the Performance Management Committee members:

Lois Alston	Harriet Greene	Pam Powell
Keisha Burns	Connie Jansen	Margee Ross
Francis Donovan	Cheryl Lantz	Maxine Simmons
Marshall Fitzgerald	Tracy Long	Valerie Wade
Jay Giles	Debbie Myers	

Appendix J

MATERIALS FOR EVALUATING THE USE OF TEACHER PORTFOLIOS

Sample Cover Letter for Evaluating the Use of Professional Teacher Portfolio

(Date)

Dear Teacher:

As you know, the use of portfolios as a key component of the teacher evaluation system in the Yourtown Schools was implemented this school year. Preliminary reports regarding the use of portfolios are promising and we hope that you are finding their use a valuable addition to the evaluation system.

Although we conducted an extensive review of research regarding teacher portfolios and piloted their use in Yourtown Schools for some time before actually implementing them division-wide, we would like to verify how well they are working. Therefore, we are asking you to participate in a follow-up study related to determining the effectiveness and efficiency of portfolio use. Specifically, we would like you to complete the enclosed survey. We plan to contact a subgroup of teachers in the future to participate in focus group meetings and further explore your experiences with portfolios.

Participation in the study is completely voluntary. Additionally, we want to assure you that the information gained from the study will be tabulated in a manner to guarantee anonymity.

Thank you in advance for your consideration and assistance. If you have any questions or concerns, please do no hesitate to contact an Evaluation Team member. And, again, thank you!

Sincerely,

Evaluation Team Leader
Yourtown Public Schools

Use of Portfolios in Personnel Evaluation
Yourtown Schools

As you know, portfolios play a key role in the new teacher evaluation system. At this early stage in implementing the new evaluation system, we would like to ask you to take a few minutes to share your perceptions regarding the use of portfolios in your evaluation.

Instructions: Please identify your position in the school district and then respond to the three questions that follow. Please return the questionnaire to the central office in the envelope provided.

Position: _____ Classroom teacher

_____ Specialist

_____ Other position (Please specify): _____

1. What are your initial impressions regarding the use of portfolios in the evaluation process?

    Positive _____   Neutral _____   Negative _____
    Comments:

2. Do you believe the use of portfolios will enhance your professional growth?

    Yes _____ Undecided _____   No _____
    Comments:

3. Do you believe the use of portfolios will provide more accurate information about your performance as a professional educator than observation alone?

    Yes _____ Undecided _____   No _____
    Comments:

Focus Group Questions: Perceived Value of Portfolios
Yourtown Schools

♦ Accuracy

- Do portfolios provide evidence of performance standards not typically observable in the classroom? In what ways?

- Are portfolios an accurate and reliable measure of teacher performance? How so?

♦ Fairness

- Are portfolios a fair means of evaluating teacher performance of professional responsibilities? How so?

- Do portfolios promote collegiality between teachers and administrators? In what ways?

- Do portfolios promote collegiality among teachers? In what ways?

♦ Usefulness

- Are portfolios a useful means for teachers to demonstrate their performance of professional responsibilities? How so?

- Does the development of a portfolio encourage reflection by teachers? In what ways?

♦ Feasibility

- Is the development of portfolios a feasible endeavor for teachers as part of the evaluation process? Why or why not?

- Is the review of portfolios a feasible endeavor for administrators as part of the evaluation process? Why or why not?

♦ General

- What are some of the advantages of using portfolios as part of a comprehensive teacher evaluation system?

- What are some of the disadvantages of using portfolios as part of a comprehensive teacher evaluation system?

Teacher Survey: Perceived Value of Portfolios
Yourtown Public Schools

Directions: Please indicate your opinion of the following statements about the use of portfolios as part of a comprehensive teacher evaluation system by placing a check in the appropriate box. The scale used includes: strongly agree (SA), agree (A), disagree (D), strongly disagree (SD), and don't know (DK). All surveys are to be completed anonymously and will be handled in a confidential manner.

Background Information: School _____ Probationary ____ Tenured ____
Years of experience w/School District _____ Total years of teaching experience _____

Fairness	SA	A	D	SD	DK
The portfolio is a fair means for me to demonstrate my performance of professional standards.					
The portfolio gives me a more prominent role in the evaluation process.					
The portfolio promotes two-way communication between my administrator and me.					
The portfolio improves my collegial relationships with administrators.					

Usefulness	SA	A	D	SD	DK
The portfolio promotes good teaching practices.					
Development of a portfolio encourages self-reflection about my work.					
Development of a portfolio helps me to think differently about my work as a teacher.					
Development of a portfolio encourages me to change instructional practices.					
Development of a portfolio assists me in identifying areas of strength and weakness.					

Feasibility	SA	A	D	SD	DK
The time required to review portfolios by administrators is reasonable.					
The time required by me to develop a portfolio is reasonable.					
The portfolio is a practical strategy for me to demonstrate my performance of professional standards.					
The portfolio offers additional substance for discussion at the evaluation review conferences.					

Please answer the remaining questions on the back of this sheet.

Accuracy	SA	A	D	SD	DK
The portfolio is a means to provide evidence of my fulfillment of professional standards not readily observable.					
The portfolio helps the principal to know me better.					
The portfolio is an accurate reflection of my performance of professional standards.					
The portfolio provides a richer and more comprehensive picture of my performance of the professional standards.					

General

1. To what degree did your principal use portfolios in evaluating your performance under the new evaluation system?

    A great deal _____   Somewhat _____   A little _____   Not at all _____

    Comments:

2. To what degree did preparing a portfolio promote your professional development?

    A great deal _____   Somewhat _____   A little _____   Not at all _____

    Comments:

3. To what degree did the former observation-only evaluation system contribute to your professional growth?

    A great deal _____   Somewhat _____   A little _____   Not at all _____

    Comments:

4. What are the major advantages of portfolios in the evaluation process from your perspective?

5. What are the major disadvantages of portfolios in the evaluation process from your perspective?

Please return to _____ by _____
            (name)   **(date)**

Administrator Survey: Perceived Value of Portfolios

Yourtown Public Schools

Directions: Please indicate your opinion of the following statements about the use of portfolios as part of a comprehensive teacher evaluation system by placing a check in the appropriate box. The scale used includes: strongly agree (SA), agree (A), disagree (D), strongly disagree (SD), and don't know (DK). All surveys are to be completed anonymously and will be handled in a confidential manner.

Fairness	SA	A	D	SD	DK
The portfolio is a fair means for teachers to demonstrate their performance of professional standards.					
The portfolio gives teachers a more prominent role in the evaluation process.					
The portfolio promotes two-way communication between teachers and me.					
The portfolio improves my collegial relationships with teachers.					

Usefulness	SA	A	D	SD	DK
The portfolio promotes good teaching practices.					
Development of the portfolio encourages teachers to reflect on their work.					
Development of the portfolio encourages teachers to think differently about their work as teachers.					
Development of the portfolio encourages teachers to change their instructional practices.					
Portfolios assist in identifying teachers' areas of strength and weakness.					

Feasibility	SA	A	D	SD	DK
The time required by me to review portfolios is reasonable.					
The time required by teachers to develop portfolios is reasonable.					
The portfolio is a practical strategy for teachers to use in demonstrating their performance of professional standards.					
The portfolio offers additional substance for discussion at the evaluation review conferences.					

Please answer the remaining questions on the back of this sheet.

Accuracy	SA	A	D	SD	DK
The portfolio is a means for teachers to provide evidence of professional standardsnot readily observable.					
The portfolio helps me to know teachers better.					
The portfolio is an accurate reflection of each teacher's performance of professional standards.					
The portfolio provides a richer and more comprehensive picture of each teacher's professional standards.					

General

1. To what degree did you use portfolios in evaluating the performance of teachers under the new evaluation system?

    A great deal _____   Somewhat _____   A little _____   Not at all _____

    Comments:

2. To what degree do portfolios promote the professional development of teachers in your building?

    A great deal _____   Somewhat _____   A little _____   Not at all _____

    Comments:

3. To what degree did the former observation-only evaluation system contribute to the professional growth of teachers in your building?

    A great deal _____   Somewhat _____   A little _____   Not at all _____

    Comments:

4. What are the major advantages of portfolios in the evaluation process from your perspective?

5. What are the major disadvantages of portfolios in the evaluation process from your perspective?

Please return to _____ by _____
                        (name)   **(date)**